JAMES MᶜNAIR's
FISH
COOKBOOK

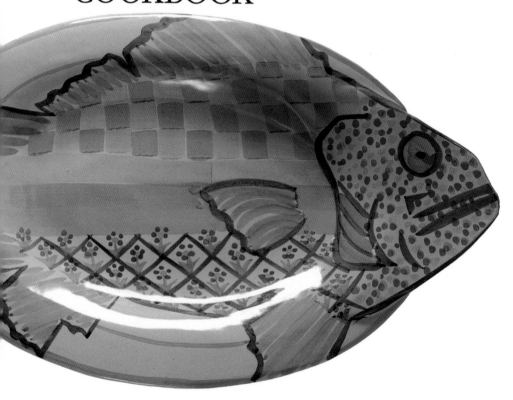

Photography and Styling by James McNair

Chronicle Books • San Francisco

Printed in Japan

Library of Congress
Cataloging-in Publication Data
McNair, James K.
[Fish cookbook]
James McNair's Fish Cookbook/
photography and styling by James McNair
p. cm.
Includes index.
ISBN 0-87701-827-8 (cloth).
ISBN 0-87701-821-9 (pbk.)
1. Cookery (Fish)
I. Title
II. Title: Fish Cookbook
TX747.M232 1991
641.6'92—dc20   91-22749
                                          CIP

Distributed in Canada by
Raincoast Books
112 East Third Avenue
Vancouver, British Columbia V5T 1C8

10 9 8 7 6 5 4 3 2 1

Chronicle Books
275 Fifth Street
San Francisco, California 94103

For my sister, Martha McNair, with whom I shared countless platters of fried catfish back in Louisiana. We now live only blocks apart in San Francisco, where that tradition continues. It has been said that you can't pick your relatives but you can select your friends. I feel fortunate to have chosen my sister as one of my closest friends.

Produced by The Rockpile Press, San Francisco and Lake Tahoe

Art direction, prop and food styling, and book design by James McNair

Editorial production assistance by Lin Cotton

Editorial, styling, and photographic assistance by Ellen Berger-Quan

Kitchen assistance by Diane Quan

Typography and mechanical production by Cleve Gallat and Samantha Schwemler of CTA Graphics

CONTENTS

INTRODUCTION

Some of my most vivid childhood memories are of lazy summer afternoons spent on the banks of Black River, Tew Lake, Bushley Bayou, and other favorite fishing holes around Catahoula Parish in northern Louisiana. My parents and I, often accompanied by various aunts and uncles, grandparents, cousins, and friends, would eagerly bait hooks dangling from long cords attached to bamboo poles, then patiently wait for the bobbing corks to be pulled under as a signal that supper was on its way. When we youngsters were bored with waiting for the fish to bite, we'd gather Spanish moss from the overhanging trees and make costumes; later we would regret the dressing up, as the tiny chiggers trapped in the moss began to bite.

Late in the afternoon, we'd build a fire or set up the folding stove. Then Daddy would heat oil in a large cast-iron pot and cook up what appeared to be a mountain of bream, perch, bass, or catfish, all to be eaten with fried potatoes and hush puppies, followed by icy watermelon or Mamma's fabulous lemon meringue pie.

After my sister, television, and junior-high school came along, there seemed to be less time for these idyllic romps and repasts under moss-laden cypresses. I've not fished much since those happy days. My family began buying catfish from a local fisherman, or Daddy would go off with his buddies and bring home a mess of fish. Nowadays when I travel to the South, we enjoy delicious catfish at the rustic Fish Fin on the outskirts of Jonesville, or travel to nearby Natchez to eat that same uniquely southern treat at The Cock of the Walk down on the muddy banks of the Mississippi.

Whenever I fry up catfish (now farm-raised near my old fishing holes and shipped everywhere) back home in San Francisco or on the northern shore of Lake Tahoe, I am transported to those simpler times spent on the banks of Louisiana's myriad waterways. Somehow fish has never again tasted quite so scrumptious!

Although southern-style deep-fried catfish remains my sentimental favorite, I've happily expanded my experiences to include fish harvested from the Gulf of Mexico, the Atlantic, the Pacific, the Mediterranean, the Aegean, and the freshwater streams and lakes of North America. Those discoveries are reflected in the pages that follow.

FRESHWATER AND SALTWATER FISH

The recipes in this collection may be used for fish caught in fresh water or salt water, as well as for those that are born in fresh water, travel into the oceans to mature, and then return to spawn in fresh water. The latter group, which are known as anadromous fish, include such well-known species as salmon, smelt, steelhead trout, and shad. In contrast, catadromous fish such as eel live in fresh water and go to the sea to spawn.

Whether a fish comes from the ocean or a nearby body of inland water, the most important thing to keep in mind is that it must be absolutely fresh. In some cases, this will mean that the fish has been cleaned promptly after catching, then frozen for shipment. Although freezing robs fish of moisture, the rapid onset of deterioration once fish is out of water sometimes calls for sacrificing some moisture for freshness.

OPPOSITE: *For deep-fried catfish in the style of the Old South, follow the recipe on page 48, omitting the red pepper from the coating mix. For hushpuppies, use a favorite recipe or refer to* James McNair's Corn Cookbook.

Cleaning

A CLEAN PURCHASE

When you purchase fish from a reliable fishmonger—the only safe source for buying fish—it will be already properly cleaned and ready to cook. If there is any doubt about the quality of your source, carefully read through this section to learn how to check fish to be sure that it was properly cleaned.

NUTRITION AND HEALTH

A growing body of reputable medical research supports the claim that the omega-3 fatty acids found in fish may help lower blood cholesterol levels in humans, thereby aiding in the prevention of strokes and heart attacks. Other studies indicate that these same fatty oils may assist in staving off a host of additional medical problems, including arthritis and breast cancer.

Fish that live in cold waters develop more of these polyunsaturated fatty acids than the species that inhabit warmer waters. The highest amounts of omega-3 are found in albacore tuna, anchovy, bluefish, eel, herring, lake trout, mackerel, mahi-mahi, sablefish, salmon, sardine, and whitefish.

The tastiest fish is the one you hook yourself. For the fullest flavor, only a few hours should pass between the catch and the cooking. As soon as the fish is out of the water, kill it with a sharp blow to the head, then make a small deep cut behind the anal opening and drain off as much blood as possible. Even at this point the digestive enzymes will continue to work, causing the fish to spoil, so clean the fish immediately, if possible, and place it on ice. If this is inconvenient, place it on ice and clean it within a couple of hours.

To clean a fish, place it on a cutting board large enough to hold the entire fish comfortably. If the catch is too big for available boards, cover a kitchen counter or other flat surface with several thicknesses of newspaper and top the newspaper with butcher paper or white freezer wrap. Lay the fish down on its side with the stomach facing you. Insert a small, sharp knife in the anal opening and cut along the middle of the stomach all the way to the head. Be careful not to pierce the entrails as you cut. Spread the cavity open and pull out and discard the entrails, or viscera, grabbing them at the neck and pulling downward. If you are cleaning a female cod, herring, salmon, shad, sturgeon, or whitefish, and the time of year is right, look for 2 elongated sacs of roe. Remove this delicacy and place it on ice; cod and shad roe are usually panfried, the others eaten as caviar.

When I am going to serve a fish whole, I prefer to leave the fins on so that it looks normal. Fish fins can, however, be quite sharp, so you may choose to cut them off with heavy-duty shears or a sharp knife and discard them before proceeding.

With the exception of a few scaleless fish, including catfish, monkfish, and swordfish, and of those fish with minuscule scales, such as mackerel, the scales must be removed if the skin will be left on during cooking. Any fish that is going to be skinned and filleted does not, of course, need to be scaled. Scraping the scales off can be a messy job, with the little silvery disks flying in all directions. Scaling the fish inside a plastic bag makes for easier cleanup. Using a special scaling knife or the dull side of a kitchen knife and holding the fish by the tail, remove the scales by scraping along the skin on one side of the fish from the tail toward the head; then turn the fish over and scale the other side. Rinse the fish under cold running water, sliding your fingers over the whole body to locate any scales that may have been missed and removing them.

If you plan to cook the fish **whole,** you will probably want to leave the head and tail intact for a showy presentation. The gills must always be taken off, however, as they trap blood and bacteria and can ruin the flavor of the fish during cooking. To remove the gills, lift up the gill covers and cut the gills horizontally to loosen them from the head, then cut them loose at either end. Use a dish towel or folded paper toweling to grab the gills and pull them out, as they can be quite sharp and you may otherwise be cut during the pulling. Discard the gills; do not add them to the stockpot as they will turn the broth bitter. A gutted and scaled fish with the gills removed but the head and tail intact is referred to as a **whole-dressed** or **dressed** fish.

To serve a fish without its head and tail, or **pan-dressed,** first position the knife behind the pectoral fins (the fins at the base of the head) and cut along the bone that runs behind the gill openings. Then, cut through the backbone to sever the head completely. Dispose of the head or save it for making fish stock; be sure to remove the gills, as described in the previous paragraph, before adding the head to the stockpot. To remove the tail, cut it off at the point just above where it joins the body.

Position the fish in the sink, tail end up. Wash the fish very thoroughly but quickly under running cold water. Pat dry inside and out with paper toweling before cutting up, storing, or cooking.

The head (minus the gills), bones, fins, and skin, known as the **frames** of the fish, can be saved for making stock. Wash them thoroughly before using.

In addition to their omega-3 benefits, fish are rich in protein and contain a good balance of phosphorus and calcium, which is important in the prevention of bone deterioration. They are also a source of iron and vitamins A and D.

Fish are low in both sodium and calories. They are also easy to digest because they have very little connective tissue to be broken down.

Those concerned about reported chemical contaminants concentrated in fish fat should be relieved to know that strict, continuous governmental monitoring of the fishing industry ensures that the fish currently being marketed through reliable outlets come from clean waters.

Cutting Fillets and Steaks

BONING

There are times when you will want to bone out a whole fish or a fish section for stuffing. Both round and flat fish are boned in the same way.

To remove the bones from a dressed fish or fish section, lay the fish on its side and, with a sharp, flexible-bladed knife, extend the cavity opening from the base of the head to the beginning of the tail. Next, insert the blade into the cavity at the head end, so that the blade rests on top of and perpendicular to the backbone. Cut along the top side of the backbone to the tail end, stopping just short of the tail and being careful not to cut through the flesh and skin along the back of the fish.

Turn the fish over, insert the knife into the cavity in the same manner, and again cut along the backbone from the head to the tail end. With the knife still inside the cavity, cut through the backbone where it joins the head and where it joins the tail. Gently pull the backbone from the cavity, using the knife as needed to free it. Pull out any remaining bones with tweezers or needle-nosed pliers.

Fish come in two anatomical forms: *round* fish, which account for the vast majority of fish species, and *flat* fish, a small group that includes dab (sand and sea), flounder, fluke, halibut, sole (Dover, English or lemon, petrale, rock), and turbot. Flat fish are oval, have compressed bodies, swim with their bodies horizontal to the water, and have both eyes on the same side of their heads. The dark skin that always covers their top sides blends in with the bottom of the sea where they live, helping to camouflage them from predators. Round-bodied fish may be shaped as the name implies or may be compressed, such as a pompano. They swim with their bodies vertical to the water and they have an eye on each side of their head.

To cut a whole-dressed or pan-dressed fish into whole fillets, begin with the dark top side of a flat fish or either side of a round fish. Lay the fish down with the backbone facing up and the head end positioned toward the hand you cut with. Using a very sharp boning knife and following the line of the head just behind the gill cover and pectoral fin (the fin nearest the cheekbones), cut down to the backbone. Next, cut through the flesh just above the tail. Grasping the flesh on top of the fish, insert the knife at the head end of the fish with the blade parallel to the backbone. Cutting just above the dorsal fin (the long row at the top of the fish's body), make a shallow slice along the backbone to the tail end. Following this same line and keeping the knife barely touching the bones, cut with long, smooth strokes down to the backbone of the fish. Fold the flesh back and continue cutting from the backbone over the rib bones. (When filleting a round fish, you may need to curve the knife upward slightly to keep in contact with the bones.) Do not free the fillet completely on the stomach side. Reposition the fillet (to provide bulk underneath the bones), turn the fish over, and repeat the same procedure. Now cut through the skin to free and remove both fillets. Run a finger over the fillet near the head end. If you locate any pin bones (a row of bones that extend outward at a right angle from the backbone), use a pair of tweezers or needle-nosed pliers to extract them, pulling them toward the head end of the fish. If there are large pin bones that can't be pulled out, cut them loose from the fillet on each side of the bones.

To remove the skin from a fillet, place the fillet skin side down on a firm surface. At the tail end, hold the blade of a chef's knife at a 45-degree angle and cut down to the skin but not through it. Grasp the tail skin tightly and cut, holding the knife almost flat and gently moving it back and forth in a sawing fashion, along the skin beneath the flesh; be careful not to cut through the skin.

To divide whole fillets of round fish into individual servings, cut crosswise on the diagonal to balance the thin tail section with the fleshier center portion, thereby producing pieces of uniform thickness. To divide flatfish fillets, cut into two pieces along the natural line running lengthwise down the middle of the fillet.

To cut steaks from a dressed round fish, slice the fish crosswise into equal widths, usually between ¾ and 1¼ inches. For smaller appetites, divide steaks in half by cutting along either side of the center, or dorsal, bone (discard the bone).

To form steaks with a dorsal bone into boneless servings, remove and discard bone as above. Form the two pieces of boned fish into one disk, wrapping the small end of each half around the large center section of the other half. Secure with toothpicks. If poaching, wrap each portion in cheese cloth and tie with white cotton string to keep the fish intact during cooking.

To cut steaks from a dressed flat fish, cut down to the backbone with a large, sharp knife or a cleaver, then "hammer" the knife through the bone by tapping the knife with a mallet; keep the steaks no more than ½ inch thick. Huge round fish such as shark or tuna and flat fish such as halibut are best cut by professionals.

BUTTERFLYING

Butterflying allows fish to be spread out for faster and more even cooking. It is a good way to prepare large fish such as salmon for grilling.

To butterfly a pan-dressed whole fish or a section of a large fish, follow the directions for boning in the sidebar on the opposite page. Discard the bone and spread the 2 halves of the fish or fish section out flat.

To butterfly single servings of skinned fillet, slice the fillet across the grain into pieces about 2 inches thick. Cut against the grain horizontally about three fourths through the middle of each piece; be careful not to slice all the way through. Spread the 2 halves out flat.

Shopping

The amount of fish you will need to buy or cook varies, of course, with the appetites of the diners. As a general rule, the following amounts should be sufficient.

WHOLE-DRESSED (cleaned): Allow 12 ounces per serving.

PAN-DRESSED (cleaned, with head and tail removed): Allow 8 to 12 ounces per serving.

STEAK (crosscut slices with bone) and ROAST (sections with bone): Allow 10 ounces per serving.

FILLET, BONED STEAK, BUTTER-FLIED WHOLE FISH, and BONED ROAST: Allow 8 ounces per serving.

Hooking our own fish isn't always possible. Those who live near a large city Chinatown can select live fish from tanks. Most of us rely on a fish market or supermarket where fish are sold whole, either whole-dressed (cleaned) or pan-dressed (cleaned with head and tail removed); cut into large chunks, or sections, that are sometimes called roasts; sliced crosswise into steaks; and as boned sides, or fillets, either whole or in pieces.

Careful inspection will reveal whether a fish that is advertised as fresh actually meets that description. When shopping for a whole fish, never buy one that has not already been cleaned, no matter how fresh the salesperson assures you it is. Any fish should have been cleaned sooner than the time it takes to reach retail shelves.

Begin the check with your nose. A fresh fish should have a mild odor; if it smells fishy, pass it by. Unfortunately, cut-up fish is often sold already wrapped in plastic. When you have no choice but to buy prepackaged fish, be sure the outlet is reliable, and don't hesitate to return the fish immediately upon opening if it has a foul odor.

The skin of a fresh fish is shiny; that of a fish past its prime is dull. Any fat that shows along the edges of the skin side of steaks or fillets should be white or pink. If the fat has a brownish tone it means that it has oxidized, an indication that the fish has been kept too long.

Next, check the scales, if they are still intact. They should have a bright silvery cast and glisten in the light. If a fish has not been scaled by the supplier and more than a few scales are missing, it is a sign that the fish was improperly handled at some point enroute to the market and should be avoided. Likewise pass up fish with gills that are turning either brown or light colored; they should be deep red. Eyes should protrude and be bright and clear, with shiny, dark pupils.

The flesh of a fresh fish is firm and elastic and springs back when pressed with a fingertip. It also clings tightly to the bone. Look inside the stomach cavity of a whole fish to be sure it is smooth; skip over those with any trace of blood or entrails, bones that separate easily from the flesh, soft flesh, or darkened areas. Rough texturing of the membrane along the ribs, known as belly burn, indicates that the entrails were pierced during cleaning, causing stomach enzymes to leak and begin breaking down the flesh.

Storing

As soon as you bring fresh fish into the kitchen, wash it quickly but thoroughly under cold running water and pat dry with paper toweling. An exception to this rule is tuna; the richly colored flesh turns white upon contact with water, so it is best just to pat it dry. If you purchased a whole fish, check it over to be sure the gills and all entrails were properly removed as described on page 6. If not, finish the trimming and rewash the fish.

If you must store a whole fish, place it in a colander and pack crushed ice all around the fish, cover loosely with plastic wrap, and set the colander in the coldest part of the refrigerator over a container to catch the melting ice; store no longer than 2 days. Enclose rinsed and dried fish pieces in a roomy plastic bag, place them in a container and cover loosely with plastic wrap, or wrap loosely in butcher paper. Store in the coldest part of the refrigerator for no more than 24 hours. For longer storage, freeze fresh fish as soon as you bring it home.

To freeze your own fresh fish, place steaks or fillets in heavy-duty plastic freezer bags or containers and add cold water to immerse the fish completely. Or tightly wrap whole fish or fish pieces in moistureproof plastic wrap or aluminum foil, pressing the wrapper to force out as much air as possible. Date the package and position it in an uncrowded area in the freezer. Flavor is best if the fish is cooked within 2 months, although it can be frozen for up to 4 months.

To thaw frozen fish, place the unopened package in a bowl in the refrigerator until defrosted. Bacteria grow too rapidly to thaw fish at room temperature. When the fish has defrosted, quickly rinse and dry it, as you would fresh fish. Thawed fish should be used within 24 hours.

BUYING FROZEN FISH

If you must purchase frozen fish, be sure the label reads "fresh frozen," which means that when the fish was killed it was immediately bled, cleaned, and flash-frozen. The entire fish should be frozen solid; there must be no soft spots. If you wish to keep your purchase frozen, place it in the home freezer as soon as possible; it must not thaw even slightly.

Packages of frozen fish, whether purchased or frozen at home, should be frost-free; frost is a telltale sign that temperature changes have occurred during storage or that the fish has been around too long. The flesh should never be discolored or appear dried out.

Most states require that a retail package containing fish that has been previously frozen and is being sold thawed to be labeled accordingly. It is unsafe to ever refreeze fish. You can, however, refreeze fish once it has been cooked.

Cooking

Soft-Fleshed Fish

Low-fat (less than 5%):
Drum (salt water)
Flounder (salt water)
Fluke (salt water)
Kingfish (salt water)
Redfish (salt water)
Sand dab (salt water)
Sea trout (salt water)
Skate (salt water)
Sole: English or lemon, rex (salt water)

Moderate-fat (5 to 10%):
Bluefish (salt water)
Herring: Atlantic (salt water)

High-fat (over 10%):
Herring: Pacific (salt water)

Whether from the salty seas or fresh water, fish can be grouped into three categories that are defined by the texture of the flesh after cooking: *firm, flaky,* and *soft*. Within each of these groups are fish that are richer in fat, but even the highest-fat species are still fairly low in fat when compared to meats.

In the recipes in this book, I have chosen not to call for specific fish varieties. Instead, I want you to select the freshest fish available within the categories outlined above. For example, many recipes simply call for a firm-fleshed or flaky-fleshed fish of your choice. In fact, most fish can be adapted to any cooking method, although a few broad guidelines should be followed. Fish rich in fat are ideal for broiling and grilling, but should probably be omitted from the stockpot, as a high oil content is undesirable in delicate fish stocks and soups. Low- and moderate-fat fish may be successfully cooked by any method, but they will need to be brushed with oil or butter before grilling or broiling to prevent their flesh from drying out.

Soft-fleshed fish are best when prepared by a method that doesn't require much turning or moving during cooking. These would include baking and steaming.

Whichever type of fish you choose, be careful not to overcook it. Generally, the less fat a fish contains, the quicker it will cook, so that a soft-fleshed fish cooks extremely rapidly. Simply adjust the suggested cooking time to fit the type of fish you are preparing.

For far too long, recipes have instructed readers to test fish for doneness by flaking it with a fork. What constitutes perfectly cooked fish is, of course, a matter of personal taste, but for me—and for a lot of other good professional and home cooks—fish is overcooked by the time it flakes easily.

A better indication of doneness is to note the moment at which the flesh changes from translucent to opaque. To test for opaqueness, insert a sharp knife into the thickest part of the fish and gently pry the flesh apart so that you can see it. Another testing method calls for inserting a slender wooden skewer or the tines of a fork into the fish at the thickest part. The fish is ready if the skewer or fork meets very little resistance as it enters.

Generally speaking, fish will be done but not dried out if it is cooked for about 10 minutes per inch of thickness, measured at the thickest part; if you prefer moister fish, reduce the suggested cooking time. Cooking time also varies with the intensity of the heat.

Remember, fish continues to cook once it is removed from the heat source because of retained heat. It is preferable to have the fish still a little underdone near the bone or center than to have it dried out and tasteless from overcooking.

Flaky-Fleshed Fish

Low-fat (less than 5%):
Anchovy, fresh (salt water)
Bass: black sea (salt water) freshwater (fresh water)
Blowfish (salt water)
Bream (fresh water)
Cod (salt water)
Dab (salt water)
Gaspergoo or freshwater sheepshead (fresh water)
Haddock (salt water)
Hake (salt water)
Mackerel: king (salt water)
Mullet (salt water)
Ocean perch (salt water)
Orange roughy (salt water)
Perch (fresh water)
Pike (fresh water)
Porgy (salt water)
Redfish (salt water)
Red snapper (salt water)
Rockfish (salt water)
Salmon: pink or humpback, chum or dog (fresh water and salt water)
Sea dab (salt water)
Smelt (fresh water and salt water)
Sole: gray or witch flounder, petrale, rock (salt water)
Sunfish (fresh water)
Tilefish (salt water)
Wolfish (salt water)

Moderate-fat (5 to 10%):
Butterfish (salt water)
Croaker: spot (salt water)
Mackerel: Spanish (salt water)
Salmon: Atlantic species, Pacific coho or silver (fresh water and salt water)
Sardine (salt water)
Turbot: Greenland (salt water)
Whitebait, common name for many minnow-sized fish such as silversides or jack smelts and sand lances (fresh water and salt water)
Whitefish (fresh water)

High-fat (over 10%):
Mackerel: Atlantic and Pacific (salt water)
Sablefish (salt water)
Salmon: Chinook or king (fresh water and salt water)
Shad (fresh water and salt water)
Trout: lake (fresh water)

Firm-Fleshed Fish

Low-fat (under 5%):
Bass: sea (salt water), striped (salt water or freshwater farmed)
Blackfish (salt water)
Catfish (fresh water)
Croaker (salt water)
Grouper (salt water)
Halibut (salt water)
Jack (salt water)
Lingcod (salt water)
Mahi-mahi or dolphinfish (salt water)
Monkfish (salt water)
Sea robin or gurnard (salt water)
Shark (salt water)
Sheepshead (salt water)
Sole: Dover (salt water)
Spotted sea trout (salt water)
Sturgeon (salt water or freshwater farmed)
Swordfish (salt water)
Tilapia (fresh water and salt water)
Tuna: most species (salt water)

Moderate-fat (5 to 10%):
Amberjack (salt water)
Bonito (salt water)
Carp (fresh water)
Pompano (salt water)
Tuna: albacore (salt water)
Yellowtail (salt water)

High-fat (over 10%):
Buffalofish (fresh water)
Eel (salt water and fresh water)
Sturgeon (fresh water)

RAW & PRESERVED

Even those who think they will not enjoy raw fish may find delight in a nibble of good caviar. Federal law dictates that only the prized eggs, or roe, of sturgeon may be marketed as caviar in the United States. The roe from any other fish must be labeled as to the type of fish. But in practice, we call all prized fish eggs caviar in the same way that we dub all sparkling wines champagne.

Sturgeon roe looks like gray-black pearls, and costs almost as much as jewels; it is identified by the variety of sturgeon, the most coveted of which are beluga, sevruga, and osetrova (variously spelled ossetra, osetra, and oscietre).

Salmon roe, which comes principally from the chum and coho varieties, is much larger than that of sturgeon roe and the color varies from bright red to light orange. Whitefish caviar is tiny and golden; the eggs of cod, crab, and flying fish are usually lightly tinted to enhance their natural colors. Inexpensive lumpfish roe is dyed to resemble costly sturgeon caviar.

Since antiquity and up until the advent of cold storage, fish was preserved by curing in brine, packing in salt, or smoking. These practices survive today strictly for the superb flavors they impart to the fish.

Curing fish overnight in fresh citrus juice renders one of the world's most delightful dishes. Use my seviche recipe as a starting point for adding your own special seasonings.

Salt cod is considered a delicacy in many parts of the world. Once it has been soaked and simmered to soften and eliminate most of the salt, the fish can be used in a variety of dishes that call for cooked fish.

Good smoked fish is expensive. For economy and flavor that rivals or occasionally exceeds the best imports, smoke your own fish whenever high-quality whole fish or fillets are readily available. Home smoking is not only kind to your budget, but also a great culinary adventure.

SERVING CAVIAR

Unopened fresh caviar should be used within 30 days. Its pasteurized counterpart, admittedly not as tasty as the fresh form, normally lasts up to 6 months or until a layer of thick white paste begins to form. Broken eggs, dubbed pressed caviar, are a good buy, although some people object to their slightly sticky texture and strong taste. Whichever roe you buy, store it in the coldest spot of the refrigerator or, preferably, on ice. Once opened, transfer unused caviar to airtight containers as long as 2 or 3 days for fresh, or up to 5 days for pasteurized. Pasteurized caviar tastes better if placed in a sieve and rinsed under cool water for a couple of minutes. Drain, cover, and chill before serving.

The fussiest aficionados believe that fresh caviar must be served straight from the container in which it was packed. Less rigid consumers insist on it being served in a chilled glass bowl, preferably nestled in crushed ice. In either case, the delicate eggs should be scooped with a spoon or knife made of bone, mother-of-pearl, or crystal but never metal. Accompany caviar with very thin black bread, toasted white bread slices, or thin buckwheat pancakes (blini) and, if you wish, a choice of such condiments as sour cream, minced hard-cooked egg, chopped onion or chives, fresh dill, and lemon for squeezing.

Whether it's black, red, or golden, caviar also makes a stunning garnish for fish dishes.

Carpaccio of Fish

Today's chefs have stolen the term for sliced raw beef, Italian style, for their thinly sliced raw fish dishes.

I always purchase fish for serving raw from a Japanese market that sells to sushi and sashimi chefs. Wherever you shop, be sure the fish is extremely fresh. For an attractive presentation, choose two types of fish with flesh of contrasting hues. Halibut, sea bass, red snapper, tuna, yellowtail, or other fish with moderate to high oil content are good choices. Avoid freshwater fish, which can harbor parasites that are killed when the fish is cooked. The color of salmon makes it a particularly desirable ingredient for raw dishes, but fresh salmon should be frozen for 48 hours to kill any potentially harmful parasites that the fish might have picked up during its journey into fresh waters; thaw the fish in the refrigerator.

Quickly rinse the fish under cold running water and pat dry with paper toweling. Using tweezers or needle-nosed pliers, remove any pin bones from the fish. For easier slicing, wrap the fish in plastic wrap and place in the freezer for about 30 minutes.

Just before serving, slice the fish across the grain into very thin pieces. Place each slice between two sheets of waxed paper or plastic wrap and pound with a mallet or other flat, heavy instrument until the fish is translucent and as thin as possible; be careful that it does not tear. Remove the top sheet of paper or wrap, transfer the fish to individual serving plates, and peel off the remaining sheet of paper or wrap. Cover the plate with the pounded fish, overlapping the pieces slightly.

Sprinkle the fish to taste with salt and pepper, or offer each at the table. Scatter the shallot or onion, chives, and sweet pepper over the top. Drizzle with the olive oil and vinegar or lemon juice. Garnish with the flowers (if used) and serve immediately.

Serves 4 as a starter.

8 ounces firm-fleshed or flaky-fleshed fish fillet, preferably two types with distinct color differences, skinned
Salt
Freshly cracked black pepper
4 teaspoons minced shallot or red onion
4 teaspoons minced fresh chives
2 tablespoons *each* finely diced red sweet pepper and gold sweet pepper
Fruity olive oil, preferably extra-virgin, for drizzling
Balsamic vinegar or freshly squeezed lemon juice for drizzling
Edible flowers such as allium (wild onion), borage, or viola for garnish (optional)

Seviche

1½ pounds fish fillet, skinned
1 cup freshly squeezed lime juice
3 tablespoons light olive oil or high-quality vegetable oil
⅓ cup finely chopped green onion, including some of the green tops
½ teaspoon minced or pressed garlic
½ teaspoon minced or pressed fresh ginger root
⅓ cup finely chopped fresh cilantro (coriander)
½ cup finely diced, peeled, and seeded tomato
Salt
Tabasco sauce or other liquid hot-pepper sauce

Lean white fish such as sole, snapper, or flounder are customarily used in this refreshing dish eaten throughout the Caribbean and Latin America. Almost any saltwater fish can be used. If you choose salmon or another anadromous fish, first freeze the fish for 48 hours to kill any potentially harmful parasites that the fish may have picked up when it entered fresh water; farm-raised baby salmon may be used without freezing. A mixture of several types of fish with flesh of varying colors makes a striking dish.

Quickly rinse the fish under cold running water and pat dry with paper toweling. Cut into bite-sized cubes or strips.

Place the fish in a ceramic or glass container, add lime juice, and toss well. Cover tightly and refrigerate for at least 5 hours but no more than 24 hours, stirring several times. If the fish cannot be served within a short time after 24 hours, drain off the liquid and toss the fish with a little olive oil to prevent it from drying out.

Shortly before serving, add the oil, green onion, garlic, ginger, cilantro, and tomato; stir well. Season to taste with salt and pepper sauce.

Serves 8 as a starter, or 4 as a main course.

VARIATION: For Polynesian-style cured fish, served throughout the South Pacific, stir about 1 cup freshly made or canned coconut milk into the fish with the oil and other ingredients.

Creamed Salt Cod Gratin

1 pound boneless salt cod
6 tablespoons (¾ stick) unsalted
    butter
3 tablespoons all-purpose flour
2 cups milk
2 teaspoons worcestershire sauce
Salt
Freshly ground white pepper
Tabasco or other liquid hot-pepper
    sauce
Softened butter for greasing
1 cup fresh bread crumbs, preferably
    made from French bread
1 cup grated Gruyère (about
    3 ounces) or other good-melting
    cheese
Fresh celery leaves for garnish
Pesticide-free nasturtium buds for
    garnish (optional)

This old-fashioned recipe calls for salt cod, which is very popular throughout the Mediterranean countries, Scandinavia, and the Caribbean islands. The dish can also be made with freshly cooked flaky-fleshed fish; pick up the recipe at the third step.

Place the salt cod in a shallow bowl and add cold water to cover the fish. Cover the bowl, refrigerate, and soak until the flesh is soft, from several hours to 24 hours, depending on the drying method and amount of salt used in preserving; ask your supplier to suggest soaking time. Change the water several times during the soaking process.

Drain the softened cod and place it in a saucepan. Add cold water to cover and set over medium heat. Bring to a boil, then reduce the heat to low and simmer until tender, about 10 minutes. Drain and flake the cod into bite-sized pieces.

In a saucepan, melt 4 tablespoons of the butter over medium-high heat. Blend in the flour and cook, stirring constantly, for 3 minutes; do not brown. Slowly add the milk, stirring briskly with a wire whisk or wooden spoon. Reduce the heat so the mixture simmers and continue to cook, stirring or whisking, until the sauce is smooth and thickened, about 10 minutes. Stir in the worcestershire sauce and flaked cod. Season to taste with salt, pepper, and pepper sauce.

Preheat a broiler. Butter a flat 1-quart baking dish or gratin pan, or 4 individual gratin dishes.

Spoon the cod mixture into the prepared baking dish or gratin pan, or into the individual gratin dishes. Sprinkle the top with the bread crumbs and cheese. Cut the remaining 2 tablespoons butter into small pieces and dot the pieces over the top. Place under the broiler until heated through and bubbly, about 10 minutes. Remove from the broiler, garnish with the celery leaves and nasturtium buds (if used), and serve piping hot.

Serves 4 as a starter or light main course.

Basic Smoked Fish

Although any firm-fleshed or flaky-fleshed fish can be smoked, those with a high oil content, such as bluefish, eel, mackerel, sablefish, Chinook or king salmon, freshwater sturgeon, lake trout, and whitefish, are the most successful. This recipe can also be used for smoking whole fish, fish steaks, or smaller fillet pieces. Check cooking times in the smoker manufacturer's directions.

To make the brine, combine the water, salt, sugar, and bay leaves in a large bowl; stir well.

Quickly rinse the fish fillets under cold running water and pat dry with paper toweling. Place the fish in a shallow glass or ceramic container and pour the brine over it to cover. Cover the container with plastic wrap and refrigerate for at least 3 hours or up to 10 hours. Drain the fish, rinse well in cold water, and place, skin side up and uncovered, on a wire rack until the flesh is dry, 30 minutes to 1 hour.

Preheat a smoker and add wood chips according to the manufacturer's directions. Brush the smoker rack with vegetable oil.

Place each fillet on several layers of cheesecloth or on a sheet of heavy brown paper and cut the cloth or paper into the shape of the fillet. When the temperature in the smoker reaches 170° F, place each fillet, skin side down, on the cheesecloth or paper and transfer, cloth side down, to the smoker rack. Cover the smoker and smoke the fish until it is just opaque when cut into at the thickest part with a small, sharp knife, 10 to 12 hours, or until done to preference. Restock the wood chips whenever necessary; usually about 3 pans of chips in all are needed.

Remove the fish from the smoker. Cool briefly, then peel off the cheesecloth or paper, which will probably pull the skin off with it. Serve immediately. Alternatively, cool to room temperature, cover, and refrigerate for up to 2 weeks or wrap tightly in freezer wrap and freeze for up to 2 months.

Serves 12 to 16 as a starter or light main course.

2 quarts water
1 cup salt
1¼ cups granulated sugar or firmly packed brown sugar
3 bay leaves
2 whole firm-fleshed or flaky-fleshed fish fillets, about 3 pounds *each*, with skin
About 10 cups very small hickory or other aromatic wood chips for smoking
Vegetable oil for brushing

Cucumber Potato Salad
with Smoked Fish

DILL DRESSING
1 cup crème fraîche, sour cream, or
    plain yogurt
1 cup minced fresh dill
2 teaspoons freshly squeezed lemon
    juice, or to taste
About ½ teaspoon salt
About ⅛ teaspoon freshly ground
    black pepper

1½ pounds new potatoes
Salt
Freshly ground black pepper
1 cup diced, peeled cucumber,
    preferably seedless type
½ cup minced red onion
30 thin slices (about 1 pound) boneless
    smoked fish, preferably salmon,
    trimmed into large triangles
Fresh dill sprigs for garnish

For a simpler presentation, cut the fish into small pieces and toss with the potatoes and cucumber.

To make the dressing, combine all the ingredients in a small bowl, including the salt and pepper to taste, and blend well. Set aside.

Wash the potatoes under running cold water, scrubbing well to remove all traces of soil. Place them in a saucepan, add cold water to cover by about 2 inches, and remove the potatoes. Bring the water to a boil over medium-high heat, add the potatoes, and cook until tender when pierced with a wooden skewer or small, sharp knife, about 10 minutes for tiny potatoes or 15 to 20 minutes for larger ones. Drain, return the potatoes to the pan, and set over the heat. Shake the pan until the moisture evaporates and the potatoes are dry to the touch.

Cut the potatoes into halves, quarters, or slices and place them in a bowl. Season to taste with salt and pepper. Cool slightly, then add the cucumber, onion, and dressing to taste and toss gently to mix thoroughly.

To serve, arrange five slices of the fish in a star pattern on each plate. Top the salmon with a scoop of the potato mixture and garnish with the dill sprigs.

Serves 6 as a salad course, or 3 or 4 as a main course.

Smoked Fish with Rice (Kedgeree)

3 eggs
Unsalted butter for baking dish
1 cup long-grain white rice,
    preferably basmati
2 tablespoons unsalted butter
½ cup finely chopped yellow onion
1½ cups homemade chicken stock or
    water, or ¾ cup canned chicken
    broth diluted with ¾ cup water
10 ounces boneless smoked fish,
    skinned and coarsely chopped
6 ounces flavorful smoked ham, cut
    into small dice
½ cup chopped fresh herb such as
    chervil, dill, or parsley,
    preferably flat-leaf type
3 tablespoons minced fresh chives
¼ cup (½ stick) unsalted butter,
    melted
½ cup crème fraîche or sour cream
    mixed with ¼ cup heavy
    (whipping) cream or half-and-
    half and 1 teaspoon curry
    powder, or to taste
Salt
Ground cayenne pepper
Fresh herb sprigs (same type as used
    in fish mixture)
Minced fresh chives for garnish
Mango chutney

No book on fish would be complete without this classic Anglo-Indian breakfast dish. This version is also good at lunch or supper and is a good buffet dish. Although traditionally prepared with smoked haddock (finnan haddie), I prefer a milder-tasting smoked fish such as salmon, trout, or whitefish.

Place the eggs in a saucepan and add just enough water to cover them. Place over high heat. As soon as the water begins to simmer, reduce the heat to keep the water barely simmering and cook for 15 to 18 minutes. Remove from the heat, drain the eggs, and plunge immediately into cold water to halt the cooking; set aside.

Preheat an oven to 350° F. Butter a 2-quart ovenproof dish, preferably one with a lid.

If using imported rice, spread it out on a tray or other flat surface and remove any foreign bits or imperfect grains by hand. If using domestic rice, this step may be omitted. Place the rice in a bowl and add cold water to cover. Stir vigorously with your fingertips, then drain. Repeat this procedure several times until the water is almost clear. Drain well and set aside.

Melt 1 tablespoon of the butter in a heavy saucepan over medium-high heat. Add the onion and sauté until soft but not browned, about 5 minutes. Add the drained rice and gently sauté until all the grains are well coated, about 2 minutes. Add the stock, water, or diluted broth. Bring to a boil, stir once, reduce the heat to very low, cover tightly, and simmer for 17 minutes. Remove the rice from the heat. Add the remaining 1 tablespoon butter and fluff the rice with a fork, lifting from the bottom instead of stirring, to separate the grains. Transfer the rice to a large bowl.

Add the fish, ham, chopped herb, chives, butter, and curried crème fraîche or sour cream to the rice. Season to taste with salt and cayenne pepper. Mix well and pour into the prepared baking dish. Peel the reserved eggs. Grate the eggs finely and sprinkle them evenly over the top of the rice mixture. Cover the baking dish tightly with a fitted cover or aluminum foil. Bake until heated through, about 20 minutes. Garnish with herb sprigs and minced chives and serve with the chutney on the side.

Serves 4 to 6 as a main course.

Smoked Fish Timbales

For easier preparation, serve these elegant cloud-light molds with warm Beurre Blanc (page 90) or a favorite tomato sauce. For a main course, use larger baking dishes or serve two timbales on each plate.

Preheat an oven to 350° F. Butter six 6-ounce or ten 4-ounce timbale molds and set aside.

Place the fish in the freezer for 10 minutes to chill.

Prepare the sauce and set aside; reheat gently before serving.

Coarsely chop the chilled fish in a food processor. With the motor running, slowly add the whole eggs and egg whites through the feed tube. Process for 1 minute. With the motor still running, slowly add the cream through the feed tube and blend well. Stir in the horseradish and salt and white pepper to taste. Cover the mixture and place in the freezer for 5 minutes to chill.

Spoon the chilled fish mixture into the prepared ramekins, filling each about two-thirds full. Cut out 6 rounds of waxed paper or baking parchment a little larger than the diameter of the ramekins. Butter one side of each round and loosely cover each ramekin with a paper round, buttered side down. Set the ramekins in a large pan, transfer the pan to the oven, and pour enough boiling water into the pan to reach halfway up the sides of the ramekins.

Bake until puffy and a wooden skewer inserted in the center comes out clean, about 30 minutes. Remove from the oven and let stand for 5 minutes.

To unmold each timbale, run a thin knife blade around the inside edges of the mold. Invert the timbales onto warmed individual plates and spoon some sauce over each timbale and onto each plate. Garnish the tops with the sweet pepper, lemon zest, caviar (if used), and herb blossoms (if used). Serve immediately.

Serves 6 to 10 as a starter, or 3 to 5 as a light main course.

Unsalted butter for ramekins and paper lids
1 pound boneless smoked fish such as salmon, sturgeon, or trout
Rich Wine Sauce, page 91, made with red wine
2 whole eggs, lightly beaten
2 egg whites, well chilled
¾ cup heavy (whipping) cream
2 teaspoons prepared white horseradish, drained
Salt
Freshly ground white pepper
Boiling water for baking pan
Roasted red sweet pepper, cut into decorative shapes, for garnish
Fresh lemon zest, cut into very thin julienne strips, for garnish
Caviar for garnish (optional)
Herb blossoms such as rosemary or borage for garnish (optional)

Simmered & Steamed

All of the recipes in this section call for cooking in or above liquid. These moist-heat techniques are a gentle method for preparing almost any type of fish.

Although fish may be poached in plain water, or a combination of water and dry white wine, or even milk, the traditional poaching medium known as court bouillon (page 32) imparts the most flavor; as an extra bonus, the fish may be served in some of the poaching broth. Prepare the poaching liquid in a specially designed narrow fish poacher or in any pot in which a whole fish or fish pieces will fit comfortably. Whole fish, fillets, and steaks may all be poached in the same way, either barely simmering on the stovetop or in a 375° F oven. Poached fish may be served hot, at room temperature, or chilled.

A good fish stock, made with bones and trimmings, is the basis of a successful fish soup. Avoid adding fish with a high-fat content to the pot as they will render an oily stock.

Braising, or cooking in a small amount of well-seasoned liquid, is a marvelous way to cook mild-flavored fish that benefit from a rich simmering liquid. Steaming is a healthful method for cooking fish, as the addition of fats is unnecessary. Any fish may be steamed; however, the naturally high fat content of oil-rich fish releases a particularly intense, desirable flavor during the steaming.

Warm Poached Fish
in Court Bouillon

Compound Butter (page 90), made
    with fresh herbs

COURT BOUILLON
2 quarts water
3 cups dry white wine
½ cup freshly squeezed lemon juice
    or white wine vinegar
1 cup very thinly sliced leek or finely
    diced yellow onion
1 cup finely diced carrot
1 cup finely diced celery
4 or 5 fresh parsley sprigs
2 or 3 fresh thyme and/or tarragon
    sprigs
2 fresh bay leaves or 1 dried bay leaf
2 teaspoons salt
1½ teaspoons black peppercorns,
    bruised

2 pounds firm-fleshed or flaky-fleshed
    fish fillet, with skin, cut into
    4 equal pieces about 1 inch
    thick, or 4 fish steaks, about 8
    ounces *each* and 1 inch thick
Fresh lemon zest, cut into thin
    julienne strips, for garnish
Fresh chives, cut into same length as
    lemon strips, for garnish

For best results, choose firm-fleshed or flaky-fleshed fish from the list on pages 12 and 13; avoid those with high-fat content. Use the same technique to poach whole fish (you may need additional liquid). Accompany the fish with good French-style bread for soaking up all the tasty liquid.

Prepare the herb butter and set aside.

To prepare the Court Bouillon, combine all the ingredients in a nonreactive fish poacher or pot large enough to hold the fish with plenty of extra room. Place over medium-high heat and bring to a boil. Reduce the heat to low, cover, and simmer until the liquid is full-flavored, about 30 minutes.

Quickly rinse the fish under running cold water and shake off excess water. Place the fish in the simmering liquid; if there's not enough liquid to immerse the fish, add boiling water to cover completely. Adjust the heat to maintain a very gentle simmer and poach the fish until the flesh is opaque when cut into at the thickest part with a small, sharp knife, about 3 minutes for small, thin pieces, up to 10 minutes for large, thick pieces, or until done to preference. Do not let the liquid boil; there should be only a few bubbles breaking on the surface.

With a slotted utensil, transfer the fish to a tray or plate. Carefully remove the skin, if desired; remove any protruding pin bones with tweezers or needle-nosed pliers. Reserve the poaching liquid in the pan.

Place a piece of fish in each of 4 individual shallow bowls and top each serving with a dollop of the herb butter. Quickly bring the poaching liquid to a boil and ladle about ¾ cup of the liquid over each portion of fish. Garnish with the lemon zest and chives and serve immediately.

Serves 4 as a main course.

Trio of Cold Poached Fish
with Wasabi Mayonnaise

Poached fish make an elegant and easy dish for entertaining because all of the cooking can be done in advance. I like to combine small portions of three types of fish for each serving; in the photo, I've used tuna, salmon, and sea bass. Ask your fishmonger to recommend three fresh fish species that will render three different colors when cooked.

To make the mayonnaise, combine all the ingredients in a small bowl and mix well. Refrigerate until shortly before serving.

Prepare the Court Bouillon in a nonreactive fish poacher or pot large enough to hold the fish with plenty of extra room. Keep at a simmer over low heat.

Quickly rinse the fish under cold running water and shake off excess water. Cut each type of fillet into 4 equal pieces. Place the fish in the simmering liquid; if there's not enough liquid to immerse the fish, add boiling water to cover completely. Adjust the heat to maintain a very gentle simmer and poach the fish until the flesh is opaque when cut into at the thickest part with a small, sharp knife, up to 10 minutes, or until done to preference. Do not let the liquid boil; there should be only a few bubbles breaking on the surface.

With a slotted utensil, transfer the fish to paper toweling to drain well. Remove any protruding pin bones with tweezers or needle-nosed pliers. Cool to room temperature before serving, or cool slightly, cover, and refrigerate for at least 1 hour or as long as overnight; return almost to room temperature before serving.

Arrange a piece of each type of fish on each plate. Add a dollop of the mayonnaise on the side and garnish the fish with herb sprigs and flowers (if used). Garnish the plate with chives.

Serves 4 as a main course.

WASABI MAYONNAISE
1½ cups homemade mayonnaise or high-quality commercial mayonnaise
Japanese horseradish powder *(wasabi)*
3 tablespoons minced fresh herb such as chervil, chives, or parsley, preferably flat-leaf type

Court Bouillon (page 32)
8 ounces *each* of three types of firm-fleshed or flaky-fleshed fish fillet with distinct color differences, skinned
Fresh herb sprigs such as chervil, dill, or parsley, preferably flat-leaf type, for garnish
Pesticide-free edible flowers such as borage for garnish (optional)
Whole fresh chives for garnish

Mediterranean Fish Soup

FISH STOCK
3 pounds fish heads, bones, and
    trimmings
2 cups chopped yellow onion
2 cups chopped celery
4 or 5 fresh parsley sprigs
4 fresh or 2 dried bay leaves
1 tablespoon minced fresh tarragon
    or thyme, or 1 teaspoon dried
    tarragon or thyme
1½ quarts dry white wine
1½ quarts water
1 egg white
Crushed shells of 2 eggs

Garlic Mayonnaise (page 92)
Red Pepper Sauce (page 92)
8 slices French bread, about ½ inch
    thick, or 16 slices skinny
    baguette, about ½ inch thick
4 tablespoons fruity olive oil,
    preferably extra-virgin
2 tablespoons unsalted butter
2 cups thinly sliced leek, white and
    pale green tops
1 tablespoon minced or pressed garlic
⅛ teaspoon crumbled saffron threads
1 cup chopped, peeled, and seeded
    ripe or drained canned tomato
Salt
Freshly ground black pepper
2 pounds firm-fleshed or flaky-fleshed
    white fish fillet, skinned and cut
    into large bite-sized chunks
Minced fresh parsley, preferably
    flat-leaf type, for garnish

Here I have combined elements of several classic fish soups served along the shores of the Mediterranean to create my own version. Make the flavorful stock in quantity and keep some in the freezer as a base for other soups or for sauces.

To make the stock, wash the fish parts under cold running water. Crack the heads and place them along with the other fish parts in a stockpot or large saucepan. Add all the remaining ingredients, except the egg white and eggshells, and bring to a boil over medium-high heat. Reduce the heat to low and simmer, uncovered, until the liquid is reduced to about 2 quarts, about 1 hour. Use a wire skimmer to remove any foam that forms on the surface during cooking. Strain through a fine wire sieve into a clean pan and discard the fish, vegetables, and herbs. Add the egg white and eggshells. Bring to a boil over high heat, then remove from the heat and let stand for 10 minutes. Slowly and carefully strain the liquid through a fine sieve lined with several layers of dampened cheesecloth. Set aside.

Prepare the Garlic Mayonnaise and the Red Pepper Sauce. Set aside. Preheat an oven to 350° F.

Brush the bread slices on both sides with 2 tablespoons of the oil. Place on a baking sheet and bake until golden brown and crisp, about 25 minutes.

In a stockpot or large saucepan over medium-low heat, melt the butter with the remaining 2 tablespoons oil. Add the leek, garlic, and saffron and sauté until the leek is soft but not browned, about 10 minutes. Stir in the tomato and the reserved fish stock. Season to taste with salt and pepper. Bring to a boil, then reduce the heat to low. Add the fish and cook until the fish is opaque when cut into at the thickest part with a small, sharp knife, about 10 minutes, or until done to preference.

To serve, ladle the soup into preheated bowls, add 1 or 2 slice(s) of toasted bread to each bowl and top the bread with dollops of Garlic Mayonnaise and Red Pepper Sauce. Sprinkle with parsley and serve immediately.

Serves 8 as a soup course, or 4 as a main course.

New Orleans Courtbouillon

Although redfish, red snapper, or catfish would be the fish of choice for this Creole specialty from the Big Easy, bluefish, halibut, swordfish, turbot, or yellowtail makes an equally delicious version. The name of the dish comes from court bouillon, the traditional broth for poaching fish, but in this case the spicy cooking liquid is thickened with a roux, a classic technique of southern Louisiana cuisine, and served as a sauce.

Pass good crusty bread for scooping up all of the sauce. For a more authentically New Orleans presentation, serve the stew over fluffy rice. Offer Tabasco for those who like it hotter.

In a large, heavy pot such as a dutch oven, heat the oil over medium heat. Stir in the flour, reduce the heat to very low, and cook, stirring constantly, until the roux is about the color of peanut butter, about 25 minutes. Add the yellow and green onions, sweet pepper, celery, and garlic. Cook, stirring frequently, until the vegetables are soft, about 10 minutes.

Add the tomatoes, herbs, allspice, water, wine, and lemon juice to the vegetable mixture. Season to taste with salt and black and cayenne peppers and mix thoroughly. Increase the heat to high and bring to a boil. Reduce the heat to low and simmer, stirring frequently to prevent the sauce from sticking, until thickened, 30 to 40 minutes.

Quickly rinse the fish slices under cold running water and shake off excess water. Add them to the simmering sauce and cook until the flesh is opaque when cut into at the thickest part with a small, sharp knife, about 10 minutes, or until done to preference. Ladle the fish and its sauce into shallow bowls, sprinkle with minced onion, and serve with the lemon.

Serves 6 as a main course.

½ cup high-quality vegetable oil
¾ cup all-purpose flour
2 cups chopped yellow onion
1½ cups chopped green onion, including some green tops
1 cup chopped red or green sweet pepper
½ cup chopped celery
1 tablespoon minced or pressed garlic
3 cups coarsely chopped, peeled, and seeded ripe or canned tomatoes with their juices
4 fresh bay leaves, minced, or 2 dried bay leaves, crumbled
¼ cup minced fresh parsley, preferably flat-leaf type
1 tablespoon minced fresh thyme, or 1 teaspoon crumbled dried thyme
1½ teaspoons minced fresh oregano or marjoram, or ½ teaspoon crumbled dried oregano or marjoram
½ teaspoon ground allspice
2½ cups water
1 cup full-bodied red wine
¼ cup freshly squeezed lemon juice
About 2 teaspoons salt
About 1 teaspoon freshly ground black pepper
About ½ teaspoon ground cayenne pepper
3 pounds firm-fleshed or flaky-fleshed fish fillet, skinned and cut crosswise into 2-inch-thick slices
Minced green onion, including some green tops, for garnish
Lemon halves or wedges for squeezing

Braised Fish, Italian Style

2 pounds very small fresh artichokes
(about 2 ounces *each*), one
8½-ounce package thawed
frozen artichoke hearts, or one
8½-ounce can artichoke hearts,
drained and rinsed
5 tablespoons fruity olive oil,
preferably extra-virgin
8 ounces fresh *porcini* or other wild
mushroom varieties, stems
discarded and caps thinly sliced
Salt
8 ounces *pancetta* (Italian bacon), cut
into ⅓-inch dice
1 cup finely chopped yellow onion
¼ cup finely chopped carrot
2 tablespoons coarsely chopped garlic
2 flat canned anchovy fillets, minced
2 pounds firm-fleshed or flaky-
fleshed fish fillet, skinned,
quickly rinsed under cold
running water, patted dry, and
cut into 4 equal pieces
1 cup dry white wine
1 tablespoon minced fresh thyme, or
1 teaspoon crumbled dried
thyme
1 fresh bay leaf, minced, or ½ dried
bay leaf, crumbled
Freshly ground black pepper
½ cup pine nuts, toasted
½ cup shredded fresh basil

I've chosen Italian flavorings to illustrate this cooking technique. Reconstituted dried wild mushrooms may be substituted for the fresh ones. Vary the dish by using seasonings and ingredients typical of other cuisines.

If using fresh artichokes, pull off and discard all the tough outer, dark green leaves. Cut off and discard the stems and top half of each artichoke. With a small, sharp knife, trim away any residue that remains of the dark green leaves. As each artichoke heart is trimmed, drop it into a bowl of water to prevent darkening.

Place each fresh, thawed frozen, or canned artichoke on a cutting surface and cut into slices about ⅛ inch thick.

In a sauté pan or skillet, heat 3 tablespoons of the olive oil over high heat. Add the mushrooms and sauté until tender, about 5 minutes. Season to taste with salt; set aside.

Preheat an oven to 450° F.

In a large sauté pan or skillet, heat the remaining 2 tablespoons olive oil over medium-high heat. Add the *pancetta* and cook until translucent, about 5 minutes. Add the artichokes, onion, and carrot. Cook until the onion is soft but not brown, about 5 minutes. Stir in the garlic and anchovies and cook 1 minute longer. Push the mixture to one side of the pan. Add the fish and sear until lightly browned on all sides. Transfer the fish and vegetables to an earthenware casserole or other ovenproof dish.

Pour off and discard the fat from the sauté pan. Return the pan to medium-high heat, add the wine, and cook about 2 minutes, scraping up the browned bits from the bottom and sides of the pan. Add the thyme, bay leaf, and salt and pepper to taste. Cook to heat through, about 2 minutes. Pour over the fish and vegetables.

Place the fish in the oven and cook until the fish is opaque when cut into at the thickest part with a small, sharp knife, about 20 minutes, or until done to preference. Just before the fish is done, drain off and discard any oil from the sautéed mushrooms and stir the mushrooms into the fish to heat through.

Transfer the fish with the juices and vegetables to a warmed serving platter or individual dinner plates and scatter the pine nuts and basil over the top.

Serves 4 as a main course.

Pacific Rim Steamed Fish

To present the fish as shown, stand it upright in the steamer and curve the body to simulate a swimming movement.

To make the vinaigrette, in a bowl or a jar with a cover, combine all of the ingredients. Whisk well or cover and shake to blend well. Set aside.

Pour water to a depth of about 2 inches into the pan of a large steamer. Place the pan over medium heat and bring to a boil.

Quickly rinse the fish under cold running water and pat dry with paper toweling. Using a small, sharp knife, diagonally score each side of the large whole fish in 2 or 3 places, if desired.

In a small bowl, combine the 12 cilantro sprigs, onion rings, garlic, ginger, mushrooms, and lemongrass. Spread about half of the cilantro-onion mixture on a shallow dish that will fit on the steamer rack with about 1-inch clearance between the dish and rack sides. Arrange the fish atop the cilantro-onion mixture. Scatter the remaining cilantro-onion mixture over the fish. Sprinkle the fish with the lemon or lime juice, soy sauce, and pepper to taste. Set the dish on the steamer rack positioned over the boiling water, reduce the heat so that the water is at a simmer, cover the steamer, and cook until the flesh is opaque when cut into at the thickest part with a small, sharp knife, 6 to 10 minutes for fish steaks or small whole fish, or about 15 minutes for a large fish, or until done to preference. Remove the fish from the steamer. If desired, quickly peel off and discard a portion of skin to reveal the flesh; pull out any exposed bones from the fish.

To serve, arrange the large fish on a serving platter or small fish or steaks on individual dinner plates. Spoon some of the cilantro-onion mixture around the fish and ladle some of the vinaigrette over the fish. Garnish with cilantro sprigs and serve immediately.

Serves 6 as a main course.

CILANTRO GINGER VINAIGRETTE

⅓ cup peanut oil or other high-quality vegetable oil

3 tablespoons rice wine vinegar

1 tablespoon minced or grated fresh ginger root

3 tablespoons chopped fresh cilantro (coriander)

Soy sauce, preferably tamari

Crushed Sichuan pepper or freshly ground black pepper

One 4- to 5-pound whole-dressed firm-fleshed or flaky-fleshed fish, four 10- to 12-ounce whole-dressed fish, or 4 fish steaks, about 8 to 10 ounces *each* and about 1 inch thick

About 12 fresh cilantro sprigs

1 small yellow onion, thinly sliced and separated into rings

3 garlic cloves, thinly sliced

About 12 thin slices fresh ginger root

5 dried black forest mushrooms, soaked in warm water to cover until soft, stemmed and thinly sliced

1 stalk fresh lemongrass, thinly sliced, or the freshly shredded zest of 1 lemon

¼ cup freshly squeezed lemon or lime juice

Soy sauce, preferably tamari

Freshly ground Sichuan pepper or black pepper

Fresh cilantro sprigs for garnish

Steamed Fish Fillet with Caribbean Curried Sauce

CARIBBEAN CURRIED SAUCE
2 tablespoons unsalted butter
2 tablespoons canola oil or other
    high-quality vegetable oil
1 cup chopped yellow onion
1 cup chopped gold sweet pepper
1 teaspoon minced or pressed garlic
1 tablespoon minced fresh red or
    green hot chile pepper, such as
    jalapeño
2 teaspoons high-quality curry
    powder
1 cup Fish Stock (page 36), or ½ cup
    canned chicken broth diluted
    with ½ cup water
1 cup freshly made or canned coconut
    milk
¼ cup freshly squeezed lime juice
Salt
Freshly ground black or white pepper

1 pound *each* two types of firm-
    fleshed or flaky-fleshed fish
    fillet with distinct color
    differences, skinned and cut to
    uniform thickness
Finely diced red or gold sweet pepper
    for garnish
Finely diced carrot for garnish
Finely minced fresh lime zest for
    garnish

Choose two fish that have a similar texture but are different colors, such as the king and ivory salmon shown here, to weave into a mat suggestive of the tropics.

To make the sauce, combine the butter and oil over medium-high heat. When the butter melts, add the onion and sweet pepper and cook until soft, about 5 minutes. Add the garlic, chile, and curry powder and cook for 1 minute longer. Stir in the stock or diluted broth and the coconut milk. Bring to a boil, then reduce the heat to low and simmer, partially covered, for 10 minutes. Add the lime juice and cook until heated through, about 2 minutes. Season to taste with salt and pepper. Pour the sauce through a fine sieve into a clean saucepan, pressing the vegetables against the sieve with the back of a wooden spoon to release all the liquid. Discard the vegetables and set the sauce aside, reheat just before serving.

Quickly rinse the fish under cold running water and pat dry with paper toweling. Cut each type of fish into 20 finger-width strips about 6 inches long. For each serving, place 5 of the strips of one type of fish side by side on a flat surface. Working with 5 strips of the other type of fish, interlace them, one at a time, with the strips on the flat surface, alternating the pattern as you add the next strip, to form a woven look. Repeat with the remaining fillet portions.

Pour water to a depth of about 2 inches into the pan of a large steamer. Place the pan over medium heat and bring to a boil. Place the woven fish portions on a shallow dish that will fit on the steamer rack with about 1-inch clearance between the dish and rack sides. Set the dish on the steamer rack positioned over the boiling water, reduce the heat so that the water is at a simmer, cover the steamer, and cook until the flesh is opaque when cut into at the thickest part with a small, sharp knife, 6 to 10 minutes, or until done to preference. (Because most steamers are not large enough to accommodate all of the fish portions on a single level without crowding, a steamer with stacking racks makes preparing this dish easier.)

Spoon some of the warm sauce onto each plate and place the fish on top. Sprinkle with the sweet pepper, carrot, and lime zest and serve immediately.

Serves 4 as a main course.

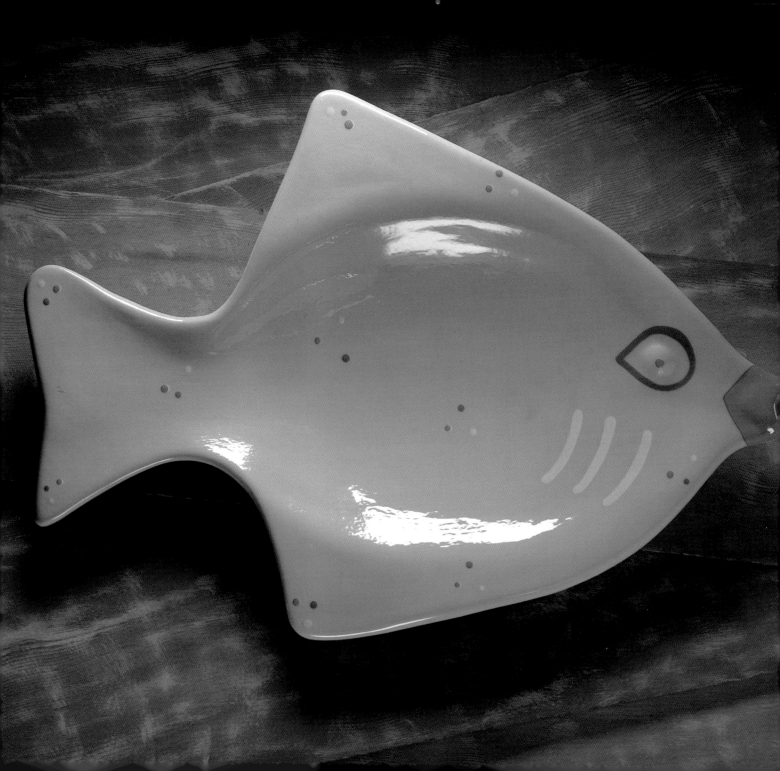

FRIED & PAN COOKED

If the cooking oil is at the right temperature, the fish will absorb very little of it during deep-fat frying. To be assured of consistently correct heat, I highly recommend a deep-fat fryer with a thermostat. In lieu of such a state-of-the-art cooker, use a heavy pot—a cast-iron dutch oven works well—and a thermometer designed for deep-frying and candy making.

Panfrying and sautéing are best done in a nonstick pan. For sautéing, be sure that the pan size allows plenty of room for the fish to be continuously moved around in the oil or fat during cooking. It is important when both panfrying and sautéing that the oil or fat be very hot before the fish is added to the pan.

Concluding this section are two other methods that require little fat and very hot pans. Blackened fish, an innovation of New Orleans chef Paul Prudhomme, has become a new American classic. The dish is marvelous when prepared properly, but I've seen far too many poor restaurant renditions. I've enjoyed numerous wok-seared fish at the modest Taraval Okazu Ya Japanese restaurant in San Francisco, where the tiny dining room is filled with smoke from the blazing woks in the open kitchen and the sizzling iron skillets on which the fish and vegetables are served. The recipe is my own version of chef Michael Yama's creation.

Spicy Deep-Fried Fish and Vegetable Chips

SPICY CORN COATING
1 cup corn flour (sometimes sold as fish fry coating)
1 cup finely ground cornmeal
About 2 teaspoons salt
About 1 teaspoon freshly ground black pepper
About ¾ teaspoon ground cayenne pepper

2 pounds whole-dressed tiny fish, four 10- to 12-inch pan-dressed fish, or 2 pounds fish fillet, skinned (cut large ones into strips about 1½ inches wide and 6 inches long)
Canola oil or other high-quality vegetable oil for deep-frying
About 6 cups thinly sliced or julienned assorted vegetables such as carrot, lotus root, summer or winter squash, and sweet potato
About 1 cup fresh parsley sprigs

OPTIONAL CONDIMENTS
Lemon wedges for squeezing
Malt vinegar for sprinkling
Ketchup
Salsa
Remoulade (page 93)
Amandine Sauce (page 91)
Old-Fashioned Tartar Sauce (page 93)

Although some people fry the vegetables in the same oil in which the fish was cooked, I prefer using two containers simultaneously. That way everything is hot when it is served and the vegetables don't taste like fish.

To make the coating, in a paper bag or plastic bag large enough to hold some of the fish, combine the corn flour, cornmeal, and salt and black and cayenne peppers to taste.

Quickly rinse the fish under cold running water and shake off excess water. Place a few pieces of the fish at a time in the bag with the coating and shake well to coat all over. Remove the coated pieces to a plate while you coat the remaining fish.

In a deep-fat fryer or a deep saucepan or dutch oven, pour in the oil to a depth of about 2 inches. Heat to 375° F. Preheat an oven to 200° F. Line a baking sheet with several thicknesses of paper toweling.

Add some of the fish to the hot oil; avoid overcrowding. Fry until the fish is golden on the outside and the flesh is opaque when cut into at the thickest part with a small, sharp knife, about 3 minutes for tiny fish, or up to 10 minutes for large whole fish or large fillets, or until done to preference. As the fish is done, remove with a slotted utensil to the paper-lined baking sheet and place in the preheated oven to keep warm. Cook the remaining fish, allowing the oil to return to 350° F before adding more fish.

Meanwhile, in a clean deep-fat fryer or other cooking pot, pour in oil to a depth of about 2 inches. Heat to 375° F. Fry the vegetables in batches until crisp, 5 to 10 minutes, depending on thickness and keep warm as in the method for the fish.

When all the fish and vegetables are cooked, drop the parsley into the hot oil in which the vegetables were cooked and cook until crisp, about 1 minute. Drain briefly. Serve the vegetables and parsley alongside the fish. Offer a choice of condiments.

Serves 4 as a main course.

Chinese Dragon Fish with Gingered Citrus Sauce

Although traditionally prepared with a whole fish, fillets make preparation and serving much easier.

To make the sauce, combine the sugar and cornstarch in a small saucepan. Stir in the boiling water and cook over low heat, stirring constantly, until thickened and clear, about 5 minutes. Remove from the heat. Add the butter, ginger, citrus juice and zest, and minced cilantro; stir until the butter is melted. Set aside.

Quickly rinse the fish under cold running water and pat dry with paper toweling. Lay the fish fillets skin side down on a flat work surface. Holding a sharp knife on a 45-degree angle, score each fillet in a diamond-shaped pattern almost through to the skin. Holding a fish fillet at both ends with the flesh side down, dip it briefly into a container of almost boiling water to shrink the meat slightly. This step will help to accent the pattern when the fillets are cooked. Repeat with the remaining fillets.

In a large deep-fat fryer or a deep saucepan or dutch oven, pour in the oil to a depth of 2 inches. Heat to 375° F, or until hot enough to brown a cube of bread within seconds. Preheat an oven to 200° F. Line a baking sheet or an ovenproof dish with several thicknesses of paper toweling.

Coat the fish on all sides with flour, shaking off excess flour. Hold a piece of the fish at both ends skin side up and carefully and slowly immerse it into the hot oil. Cook until golden on the outside and the flesh is opaque when cut into at the thickest part with a small, sharp knife, about 5 to 8 minutes, depending on the size of the fillet, or until done to preference. Remove with a slotted utensil to the paper-lined baking sheet or dish and place in the preheated oven to keep warm. Cook the remaining fish, allowing the oil to return to 375° F before adding more fish. Reheat the sauce.

Place a fish fillet on each of 4 dinner plates. Spoon a little of the sauce over and around the fish and spoon the rest into small bowls placed on each plate. Garnish the fish with the lemon or ginger slices and herb sprigs. Serve immediately.

Serves 4 as a main course.

GINGERED CITRUS SAUCE
1 cup granulated sugar
1½ tablespoons cornstarch
1 cup boiling water
2 tablespoons unsalted butter
3 tablespoons minced fresh ginger root
¼ cup freshly squeezed lemon, lime, or grapefruit juice
1 tablespoon freshly minced or grated lemon or lime zest
2 tablespoons minced fresh cilantro (coriander)

2 pounds firm-fleshed fish fillet, with skin, cut into 4 equal pieces
Water, brought almost to boiling
Canola oil or other high-quality vegetable oil for deep-frying
All-purpose flour for dredging
Lemon or pickled ginger slices for garnish
Fresh herb sprigs such as cilantro, chervil, or parsley, preferably flat-leaf type, for garnish

Marinated Fried Fish

Numerous versions of freshly fried fish topped with a hot mixture of vinegar and vegetables, then cooled before serving, have been popular throughout the Mediterranean for centuries. One of my favorite renditions comes from Venice, where fried sole is topped with a blend of vinegared caramelized onions, raisins, and pine nuts; the recipe is in my book *Cold Cuisine.* The Spanish version, *escabeche,* made its way to this side of the Atlantic, where it is known as *escovitch* or *caveach* throughout the Caribbean and tropical Latin America. In these areas, lemon or lime juice is often substituted for the vinegar.

Combine the cumin and coriander seeds in a small, heavy skillet over medium-low heat and stir occasionally until fragrant, about 3 minutes; do not burn. Add the bay leaves and oregano and heat through. Transfer the mixture to a spice grinder and grind to a powder. Set aside.

In a deep saucepan, heat the ¼ cup olive oil over medium heat. Add the onion and sauté until deep golden brown, about 10 minutes. Add the garlic and sugar and sauté 1 minute longer. Stir in the vinegar, wine, tomatoes, and the reserved spice-and-herb mixture. Bring to a boil over high heat. Reduce the heat to medium and cook until the mixture is reduced and thickened enough to almost hold its shape, about 45 minutes. Season to taste with salt and pepper.

Meanwhile, quickly rinse the fish fillets under cold running water and pat dry with paper toweling. Dredge the fillets in flour to coat lightly and shake off excess flour.

In a large deep-fat fryer or a deep saucepan or dutch oven, pour in the oil to a depth of 2 inches. Heat to 375° F, or until hot enough to brown a cube of bread within seconds. Add the fish, a few pieces at a time, and fry until golden on all sides and the flesh is opaque when cut into at the thickest part with a small, sharp knife, about 5 minutes, or until done to preference. As soon as pieces are done, remove them with a slotted utensil to paper toweling to drain. Cook the remaining fish, allowing the oil to return to 375° F before adding more fish. Sprinkle the fish to taste with salt.

Arrange the fish pieces snugly in a dish, overlapping them if necessary. Spoon the vinegar mixture over the fish. Cover loosely and let stand until cooled to room temperature. Or cover and refrigerate for 24 hours; return to room temperature before serving. Just before serving, sprinkle with the cheese (if used) and minced parsley.

Serves 4 as a main course.

1 teaspoon whole cumin seed
1 teaspoon whole coriander seed
4 fresh bay leaves, torn, or 2 dried bay leaves, crumbled
2 teaspoons chopped fresh oregano, or 1 teaspoon crumbled dried oregano
¼ cup fruity olive oil, preferably extra-virgin
1 cup chopped yellow onion
2 tablespoons coarsely chopped garlic
3 tablespoons granulated sugar, or to taste
2 cups red wine vinegar
2 cups full-bodied red wine
2 cups chopped, peeled and seeded fresh or drained canned plum tomatoes
Salt
Freshly ground black pepper
1½ pounds firm-fleshed, or flaky-fleshed lean white fish fillet, skinned and cut into 8 equal pieces
All-purpose flour for dredging
Olive oil or high-quality vegetable oil for deep-frying
1 cup (about 4 ounces) crumbled feta cheese (optional)
Minced fresh parsley, preferably flat-leaf type, for garnish

Panfried Fish

Almost any fish can be panfried, although soft-fleshed fish require particularly delicate handling. Rainbow trout or other small fish may be cooked whole; boning them before cooking makes eating them easier. For a more varied dish, cut an assortment of fish into uniform-sized pieces of the same thickness; add shellfish such as shrimp or scallops to the mix.

Quickly rinse the fish under cold running water and pat dry with paper toweling. Sprinkle to taste with salt and pepper and lightly dust with flour; shake off excess flour.

Preheat an oven to 200° F. Line a baking sheet or an ovenproof dish with several thicknesses of paper toweling.

Combine the butter and oil in a sauté pan or skillet over medium-high heat. When the butter stops foaming but is not browned, add the fish. Cook until the fish is crisp around the edges. With a wide spatula, turn the fish over and cook on the other side until the flesh is opaque when cut into at the thickest part with a small, sharp knife, 2 to 10 minutes, total cooking time, depending on the thickness of the fish, or until done to preference. Remove with a slotted utensil to the paper-lined baking sheet or dish and place in the preheated oven to keep warm. Cook the remaining fish.

Garnish the cooked fish with the herb and serve immediately with condiment of choice.

Serves 4 as a main course.

VARIATIONS: To serve the fish *à la meunière,* wipe the pan clean after frying the fish and then place the pan over medium-high heat. Add ¼ pound (1 stick) unsalted butter and heat it until it is very lightly browned. Stir in ¼ cup freshly squeezed lemon or lime juice and ¼ cup minced fresh chervil or parsley. Pour the butter mixture over the fried fish.

Four 10- to 12-ounce dressed fish, preferably boned, or 2 pounds assorted fish fillet or boned steak, cut into large bite-sized chunks
Salt
Freshly ground black pepper
All-purpose flour for dredging
¼ cup (½ stick) unsalted butter
¼ cup light olive oil or high-quality vegetable oil
Minced fresh chervil or parsley, preferably flat-leaf type, for garnish

OPTIONAL CONDIMENTS
Lemon or lime wedges for squeezing
Remoulade (page 93)
Old-Fashioned Tartar sauce (page 93)
Herbed Mayonnaise (page 92)
Compound Butter (page 90)
Amandine Sauce (page 91)

Fish Sauté with Spiced Onions

SPICED ONIONS
1 tablespoon whole coriander seed
2 tablespoons whole cumin seed
¼ cup fruity olive oil, preferably
    extra-virgin
8 cups thinly sliced yellow onions
    (about 2½ pounds unpeeled)
2 tablespoons minced or pressed garlic
2 tablespoons minced fresh ginger
    root
Salt
Freshly ground black pepper
½ cup dry white wine

2 pounds firm-fleshed or flaky-fleshed
    fish fillet, skinned
3 tablespoons unsalted butter
2 tablespoons olive oil
2 teaspoons minced or pressed garlic,
    or to taste
Salt
Freshly ground black pepper
3 tablespoons freshly squeezed lemon
    or lime juice
2 tablespoons minced fresh chives
2 tablespoons minced fresh parsley,
    preferably flat-leaf type, or
    cilantro (coriander)
Fresh parsley or cilantro sprigs for
    garnish

Quickly cooked fish rests atop a bed of slowly cooked onions in this full-flavored dish. I sometimes cut the fish into thin slices and pound them into scallops before sautéing. If time is limited, the fish is also delicious served without the onions.

To prepare the onions, combine the coriander and cumin seeds in a small, heavy skillet over medium-low heat and stir occasionally until fragrant, about 3 minutes; do not burn. Transfer to a spice grinder and grind to a powder. Set aside.

Heat the oil in a large saucepan over medium heat. Add the onions and toss well to coat with the oil. Cover tightly, reduce the heat to medium-low, and cook, stirring occasionally, until the onions just begin to color, about 30 minutes. Uncover the saucepan and add the garlic, ginger, and reserved spice mixture. Increase the heat to medium, and season to taste with salt and a generous amount of pepper. Cook, stirring occasionally, until the onions are almost caramelized, about 35 minutes. Increase the heat to medium-high, add the wine, and cook until the wine evaporates, about 3 minutes. Keep warm over very low heat, or remove from heat, cover, and reserve for several hours; reheat before serving.

Quickly rinse the fish under cold running water and pat dry with paper toweling. Slice the fish into bite-sized pieces or into strips about as wide as a finger.

In a sauté pan or skillet, preferably a nonstick pan, heat 2 tablespoons of the butter and the oil over medium-high heat until the butter stops foaming but is not brown. Add the fish and sauté, shaking the pan to keep the fish moving, until the pieces begin to turn opaque on one side, about 30 seconds; lower the heat slightly after the fish is completely seared on one side. Turn the fish and continue to cook until the flesh is opaque when cut into at the thickest part with a small, sharp knife, about 2 minutes longer, or until done to preference. Stir in the remaining 1 tablespoon butter, garlic, and salt and pepper to taste. Sauté until the butter melts, then stir in the lemon or lime juice, chives, and minced parsley or cilantro.

Spread a portion of the onions on a serving platter or individual plates and top with the fish. Drizzle the pan sauce over the fish, garnish with the herb sprigs, and serve immediately.

Serves 4 as a main course, or 8 as a starter.

Blackened Fish Fillets, à la Prudhomme

As a native Louisianian, I want to set the record straight. Blackened fish is not, as I've read so many times in recent years, an "old Cajun cooking method." The technique was developed by Paul Prudhomme, the creator of K-Paul's in New Orleans and the guru of the new-styled Cajun food that is deeply rooted in the unique cuisine of southern Louisiana.

A heavy skillet, preferably cast iron, that can withstand intense direct heat is essential for cooking blackened fish. If you wish to have all the fish ready at the same time, use two skillets for simultaneous cooking. To speed up the preparation, substitute 3 tablespoons of a commercial spice blend, such as chef Prudhomme's own mix, for the coating mix.

To make the coating mix, combine all the ingredients in a small bowl and mix well. Set aside.

Place a large, heavy skillet, preferably cast iron, over high heat until it is extremely hot and well beyond the smoking stage, about 10 minutes.

Quickly rinse the fish under cold running water and pat dry with paper toweling. Dip each piece of fillet into the melted butter to coat on both sides. Generously sprinkle both sides of each fish fillet evenly with the spice mixture and pat it onto the fish with your hands.

Place 2 pieces of the fish in the hot skillet and top each with 1 teaspoon of the melted butter. Cook until the bottom sides are very crisp and lightly charred but not burned, 1 to 3 minutes, depending on the thickness of the fish and the temperature of the skillet. Turn the fish over and top each piece with 1 teaspoon of the melted butter. Cook until the bottoms of the fish are as cooked as the first side and the flesh is opaque when cut into at the thickest part with a small, sharp knife, about 2 minutes, or until done to preference.

Transfer the blackened fish to 2 warmed dinner plates, sprinkle with the minced herbs, and place the lemon wedges and herb sprigs alongside the fish. Cook the remaining fillets. Serve the fish piping hot with melted butter (if used).

Serves 4 as a main course.

SPICY COATING MIX
1 tablespoon paprika
2 teaspoons salt
1 teaspoon *each* freshly ground black pepper and white pepper
1 teaspoon ground cayenne pepper
1 teaspoon *each* onion powder and garlic powder
½ teaspoon *each* crumbled dried oregano and thyme

½ cup (1 stick) unsalted butter, melted
2 pounds fish fillet, skinned and cut into 4 equal pieces ½ to ¾ inch thick
Minced fresh oregano and/or thyme for garnish
Lemon wedges for squeezing
Fresh oregano and/or thyme sprigs for garnish
Melted unsalted butter (optional)

Wok-Seared Fish with Stir-Fried Vegetables

1 cup soy sauce, preferably tamari
½ cup granulated sugar
¼ cup sweetened rice wine *(mirin)* or sherry
¼ cup Japanese fish stock *(dashi)* or canned chicken broth, preferably low-sodium type
2 teaspoons grated fresh ginger root
4 tablespoons peanut oil for stir-frying
4 cups bean sprouts
½ cup sliced green onion
1 cup julienned carrot, about 2 inches long
1 cup julienned snow peas
1 cup shelled fresh or thawed frozen green peas
2 pounds firm-fleshed or flaky-fleshed fish fillet, skinned and cut into 4 equal pieces about ¾ inch thick
All-purpose flour for dredging
Toasted sesame seeds
Flying fish roe for garnish (optional)

When possible, serve this Japanese-inspired dish on small cast-iron plates or skillets that have been heated to the smoking stage while the fish is cooking. Choose firm-fleshed or flaky-fleshed fish; I prefer salmon, sea bass, and orange roughy. *Mirin* and powdered *dashi* stock base can be found in Japanese markets and many well-stocked supermarkets.

In a saucepan, combine the soy sauce, sugar, rice wine or sherry, stock or broth, and ginger. Bring to a boil over high heat, stirring to dissolve the sugar. Reduce the heat to low and simmer until needed.

Pour 2 tablespoons of the oil into a wok and heat over high heat until very hot. Add the bean sprouts, green onion, and carrot and stir-fry for about 1 minute. Add the snow peas and peas and ¼ cup of the simmering soy sauce mixture. Cover the wok and cook until the vegetables are tender-crisp, about 2 minutes longer. Transfer the vegetables to a bowl and keep warm. Wipe the wok clean.

Quickly rinse the fish under cold running water and pat dry with paper toweling. Coat the fish on all sides with flour, shaking off excess flour.

Pour the remaining 2 tablespoons of oil into the wok and heat over high heat until almost smoking. Add the fish and cook on one side until golden and crispy, about 2 minutes. Turn and cook on the other side until golden and crispy and the flesh is opaque when cut into at the thickest part with a small, sharp knife, about 2 minutes longer. Transfer the fish to warmed plates and spoon the vegetable mixture alongside the fish. Ladle some of the simmering sauce over the fish and pour the rest into small bowls placed on each plate. Sprinkle the sauce with sesame seeds and garnish the fish with the roe (if used). Serve piping hot.

Serves 4 as a main course.

GRILLED & BROILED

Fish in almost any form—whole, cut into sections sold as roasts, carved into steaks or fillets, sliced into small chunks and skewered—can be grilled or broiled. When grilling whole fish, turning them will be easier if they are placed in hinged wire baskets or hinged grills. Large whole fish also look and taste great when they are cooked on a revolving spit. To assure even cooking, make a couple of incisions in the thickest part of any whole fish that is to be grilled or broiled.

Any type of fish may be successfully grilled. As soft-fleshed fish are subject to falling apart and disappearing through the grill rack, wrap them in aluminum foil with a few holes punched in it to allow the smoke to penetrate and flavor the fish.

Be sure to start with a well-scrubbed grill rack; fish easily sticks to charred remains. If cooking over coals, allow the coals to become covered with gray ash before adding the fish. Just before placing the fish on the rack or in a hinged basket, brush the metal thoroughly with vegetable oil. Small whole fish or fish pieces should be cooked fast over a fairly hot fire to sear the surface quickly and prevent the fish from clinging to the rack. To reduce further the chance of sticking, position the fish perpendicular to the grill bars so there is less direct contact. Leaving the fish in one position and turning it only once during cooking also helps minimize sticking. You may, however, wish to give the fish a 90-degree turn after searing for about a minute on the first side, to create classic crosshatched grill marks. Remove the fish from the grill *just before* it is done to your liking; it will continue to cook for a short time off the heat.

Recipes for grilling and broiling are interchangeable. To adapt a grill recipe to broiling, position the broiler rack 5 or 6 inches from the heat source. To cook in a grill pan, brush the raised ridges in the bottom of the pan with vegetable oil and preheat the pan before adding the fish.

Please check the fish section in my *Grill Cookbook* for a number of other ways to serve grilled fish.

Grilled Fish

BEAN SAUCE
1 cup white beans, covered with
    water and soaked overnight
1 tablespoon olive oil or high-quality
    vegetable oil
3 tablespoons minced shallot or red
    onion
2 teaspoons minced or pressed garlic
2 cups dry white wine
3 cups Fish Stock (page 36), or 1½
    cups canned chicken broth
    diluted with 1½ cups water
1 tablespoon minced fresh thyme, or
    1 teaspoon crumbled dried
    thyme
Salt
Freshly ground black pepper
⅓ cup cooked black beans
⅓ cup cooked red beans or pinto
    beans

4 fish steaks, about 8 ounces *each* and
    1 inch thick, 2 pounds fish fillet,
    skinned and cut into 4 equal
    pieces, four 10- to 12-ounce
    whole-dressed fish, or one 3- to
    4-pound whole-dressed fish
Olive oil or melted unsalted butter
    for brushing
Salt
Freshly ground black pepper
Vegetable oil for brushing
Fresh summer savory or other herb
    sprigs for garnish

Properly grilled fish, with its crusty exterior and tender center, needs only a squeeze of fresh lemon and a drizzle of olive oil or melted butter. To dress the fish up a bit more, I've added a bean sauce, but you should consider it optional. Canned black and red beans are acceptable additions to the sauce, or cook dried black and red beans in the same way as the white beans.

To make the sauce, drain the white beans and set aside. Heat the oil in a saucepan over medium-high heat. Add the shallot or onion and sauté until soft, about 3 minutes. Add the garlic and sauté 1 minute longer. Stir in the wine, bring to a boil, and cook until reduced by half. Add the drained white beans, stock or broth, and thyme. Bring to a boil, then reduce the heat to low, cover with a lid slightly ajar, and simmer until the beans are very tender, about 1 hour. Pour the sauce through a fine sieve set over a bowl, pressing the beans with the back of a wooden spoon to release all liquid. Place about 1 cup of the pressed beans and the liquid in a food processor or blender and blend until smooth; if too thick, add a little stock, broth, or water. Discard the remaining pressed bean mixture. Season the sauce with salt and pepper to taste. Stir in the cooked black beans and red beans. Set aside; reheat just before serving.

If cooking small whole fish, steaks, or fillets, prepare a hot fire for direct-heat cooking in an uncovered grill. If cooking a large whole fish, prepare a hot fire for indirect-heat cooking in a covered grill and place a drip pan in the center of the fire grate.

When the wood or charcoal fire is covered with gray ash or a gas grill is very hot, quickly rinse the fish under cold running water and pat dry with paper toweling. Measure the fish at the thickest point and note the measurement. Brush the fish all over with the olive oil or melted butter and season to taste with salt and pepper. Brush the inside surface of a hinged wire basket with vegetable oil and place the fish inside, or brush the grill rack with vegetable oil. Place small whole fish or pieces directly over the heat source, or position a large fish over the drip pan. Grill the fish, turning once and basting occasionally with the olive oil or butter, until the flesh is opaque when cut into at the thickest part with a small, sharp knife, about 10 minutes per inch of thickness, or until done to preference.

To serve, reheat the reserved bean sauce and ladle a portion onto each plate. Top with the grilled fish, garnish with the herb sprigs, and serve immediately.

Serves 4 as a main course.

Leaf-Wrapped Stuffed Whole Fish

Leaf wrappers are not only attractive and add subtle flavor, but they also help to keep the fish moist. Spinach, radicchio, romaine lettuce, or savoy cabbage leaves may be used in place of the grape or fig leaves.

Prepare a hot fire for direct-heat cooking in an uncovered grill.

If using fresh leaves, briefly blanch them in boiling water just until wilted. Remove immediately to a bowl of ice water; set aside. If using bottled grape leaves, rinse well under cold running water to remove the salty brine; set aside.

In a food processor or blender, combine the bread crumbs, almonds, and parsley and process just until coarsely chopped and well mixed. Add the tarragon or thyme, lemon zest and juice, and butter and mix thoroughly. Season to taste with salt and pepper.

Quickly rinse the fish under running cold water and pat dry with paper toweling. Measure the fish at the thickest point and note the measurement. Stuff the cavities of the fish with the bread crumb mixture. Skewer the fish cavities closed with toothpicks, if desired. Place the fish on a baking sheet. Pat the grape leaves with paper toweling to remove excess moisture. Wrap each fish in the leaves, overlapping them as you work. Brush all over with olive oil.

When the wood or charcoal fire is covered with gray ash or a gas grill is hot, lightly brush the inside surfaces of hinged wire baskets with vegetable oil and place the fish inside, or brush the grill rack with vegetable oil. Place the hinged wire basket or the fish directly over the heat source. Grill the fish, turning once, until the flesh is opaque when cut into at the thickest part with a small, sharp knife, about 10 minutes per inch of thickness, or until done to preference.

Meanwhile, prepare the Amandine Sauce.

Remove the fish to individual plates. Top with the sauce, sprinkle with the grapes, and serve immediately.

Serves 6 as a main course.

About 18 fresh grape or fig leaves or bottled grape leaves
Boiling water, if using fresh leaves
1 cup fine fresh bread crumbs, made from about 3 ounces good-textured bread, preferably French
1 cup unblanched almonds
1 cup fresh parsley sprigs
2 tablespoons coarsely chopped fresh tarragon or thyme leaves, or 1 tablespoon crumbled dried tarragon or thyme
3 tablespoons freshly grated lemon zest
¼ cup freshly squeezed lemon juice
6 tablespoons (¾ stick) unsalted butter, softened
Salt
Freshly ground black pepper
Six 10- to 12-ounce dressed fish, preferably catfish, salmon, or trout, boned
Olive oil for brushing
Vegetable oil for brushing
Amandine Sauce (page 91)
2 cups seedless or seeded grapes, cut in half or quartered

Jamaican Jerked Fish
with Red Pepper Salsa

Jerk is the term applied to the spicy grilled foods on the island paradise of Jamaica. The fish is rubbed with a seasoned paste before grilling. Although the mixture should be fiery to be authentic, the amount of chile pepper used can be varied according to taste. If you can't find Scotch bonnet, reputedly the world's hottest pepper, substitute jalapeño or other hot chiles.

To make the salsa, combine all the ingredients except the salt in a food processor and chop finely but do not purée. Season to taste with salt and set aside.

To make the paste, combine all the ingredients in a food processor or blender and run until smooth.

Quickly rinse the fish under cold running water and pat dry with paper toweling. Rub the fish all over with the paste and let stand until the fire is ready. Measure the fish at the thickest point and note the measurement.

Prepare a hot fire for direct-heat cooking in an uncovered grill.

When the wood or charcoal fire is covered with gray ash or a gas grill is hot, brush the inside surface of a hinged wire basket with vegetable oil and place the fish inside, or brush the grill rack with vegetable oil. Place the hinged wire basket or the fish directly over the heat source and cook, turning once, until the flesh is opaque when cut into at the thickest part with a small, sharp knife, about 10 minutes per inch of thickness, or until done to preference.

To serve, arrange the fish on individual plates or a serving platter. Spoon the salsa alongside the fish, garnish with the cilantro, and serve hot.

Serves 4 as a main course, or 6 to 8 as a starter.

RED PEPPER SALSA
3 red sweet peppers with stems, seeds, and membranes discarded, coarsely chopped
1 cup coarsely chopped, peeled, and seeded ripe tomato
¼ cup coarsely chopped shallot or red onion
2 garlic cloves, or to taste
2 tablespoons freshly squeezed lime juice
4 or 5 fresh cilantro (coriander) sprigs, coarsely chopped
Salt

JERK PASTE
½ cup chopped yellow onion
1 tablespoon chopped fresh hot chiles, or to taste
¼ cup sliced green onion, including green tops
1 teaspoon fresh thyme leaves, or ½ teaspoon crumbled dried thyme
½ teaspoon ground allspice
¼ teaspoon ground cinnamon
⅛ teaspoon freshly grated nutmeg
About 1 teaspoon salt
About ½ teaspoon freshly ground black pepper
Jamaican hot-pepper sauce (optional)

2 pounds firm-fleshed or flaky-fleshed fish fillet, skinned and cut into 12 equal pieces, or 4 fish steaks, about 8 ounces *each* and 1 inch thick
Vegetable oil for brushing
Fresh cilantro sprigs for garnish

Japanese-Style Broiled Fish

½ cup soy sauce, preferably tamari
½ cup Japanese rice wine (sake)
½ cup sweetened rice wine *(mirin)*
4 whole fish fillets, about 8 ounces
    each, with skin, or 4 fish steaks,
    about 8 ounces *each* and 1 inch
    thick
Vegetable oil for brushing
Pesticide-free Japanese maple leaves
    for garnish (optional)

Broiled fish infused with Japanese seasonings is an easy and delicious centerpiece for a simple Asian meal. Serve with fluffy rice, steamed spinach, and hot green tea, warm sake, or cold beer. The fish can also be cooked on a grill.

For an authentic dish, choose oil-rich fish such as eel, Chinook salmon, or mackerel.

In a bowl, combine the soy sauce and the rice wines to use as a marinade. Set aside.

Quickly rinse the fish under cold running water and pat dry with paper toweling. Cut each fillet into several pieces, or divide each steak into 2 pieces by cutting along either side of the central bone and then discarding the bone.

Place the fish in a shallow glass or ceramic container, keeping pieces of each fillet arranged together, and pour the marinade over the fish. Cover and refrigerate for 2 hours, turning the fish occasionally. Let the fish come to room temperature before cooking.

Preheat a broiler.

Remove the fish from the marinade, reserving the marinade. Brush a rack set in a broiling pan with vegetable oil and place the fish on the rack, skin side down; keep pieces of each fillet or steak grouped together. Position the fish 5 or 6 inches from the heat source and broil, turning once and brushing with the reserved marinade several times, until the flesh is opaque when cut into at the thickest part with a small, sharp knife, 3 to 5 minutes per side, depending on thickness, or until done to preference.

Transfer the fish, skin side up, to serving plates. Garnish with the maple leaves (if used) and serve hot.

Serves 4 as a main course.

Cajun-Style Broiled Fish

Spicy Coating Mixture (page 59) or
  commercial spice blend for fish
1 pound fish fillet, cut into 2 equal
  pieces, or 2 fish steaks, about
  8 ounces *each* and 1 inch thick
Vegetable oil for brushing
1 tablespoon minced fresh chives
2 tablespoons minced fresh herbs
  such as basil, cilantro
  (coriander), dill, or savory,
  one kind or a mixture
Cajun-style mustard or other
  favorite mustard (optional)
Fresh herb sprigs (same type as
  minced) for garnish
Lemon wedges for squeezing

Nothing could be simpler and still taste so wonderful, plus be so low in calories and fat. Any type of fish can be prepared this way; adjust the cooking time according to the thickness of the fish pieces, allowing 10 minutes per inch for opaque flesh that remains moist.

Alternatively, serve the fish with Remoulade (page 93).

Preheat a broiler. Prepare the coating mixture and set aside.

Quickly rinse the fish under cold running water and pat dry with paper toweling. Generously sprinkle both sides of the fish with coating mix, using about the same amount you would use if seasoning with salt and pepper.

Set a rack in a broiling pan and brush the rack with vegetable oil. Place the fish on the rack. Position the fish 5 or 6 inches from the heat source and broil, turning once, until the flesh is opaque when cut into at the thickest part with a small, sharp knife, 3 to 5 minutes per side, depending on thickness, or until done to preference.

Place the fish on individual plates and sprinkle with the chives and other herbs. Spoon a dollop of the mustard (if used) alongside, garnish with herb sprigs, and serve immediately. Offer lemon wedges at the table.

Serves 2 as a main course.

ROASTED or BAKED

Roasting or baking is perhaps the easiest way to cook fish. There's no grill to scrub, poaching liquid to prepare, or cold oil to dispose of. Just combine the fish with seasonings and pop it into the oven, then continue preparing the rest of the meal.

In fact, the terms *roasting* and *baking* mean the same thing—cooking by the hot, dry heat of an oven—and may be used interchangeably. I usually refer to fish that is cooked plain or with nothing more than a brushing of melted butter or oil as roasted, however. For me, baking implies that the fish is at least partially immersed in some type of liquid.

I've already included some recipes for baking in other sections of this book. In the first section of recipes, for example, are baked dishes that rely on smoked fish. Two of my braised fish dishes, although baked in the oven, seemed more appropriately included with other recipes where fish is cooked in hot liquid. Poaching, another way of cooking fish immersed in liquid, may also be done in the oven and is sometimes referred to as oven-poached or poached-baked.

No matter what you call it, oven cooking is one of the most healthful ways to prepare fish, since very little or no cooking fat is required.

Baked Fillet with
Fava Beans and Peas

If pleasantly bittersweet fava beans, or broad beans, are unavailable for this springtime dish, use lima beans or double the amount of green peas. Any white fish fillets will work well for this preparation.

Preheat an oven to 325° F.

Bring a pot of water to a boil over high heat. Drop in the fava beans and parboil for 3 to 4 minutes. Drain. Peel off and discard the thin layer of skin from each bean. Set the beans aside.

Quickly rinse the fish under cold running water and pat dry with paper toweling. Season to taste with salt and pepper. Arrange the fish pieces in a single layer on the bottom of a casserole or other ovenproof dish. Scatter the parboiled fava beans, peas, basil, and tomato over the fish. Drizzle with the oil and wine. Cover with a tight-fitting lid or aluminum foil and bake until the flesh is opaque when cut into at the thickest part with a small, sharp knife, about 10 minutes, or until done to preference. Using a slotted utensil, remove the fish to a platter and cover it with aluminum foil to keep the fish warm. Place the baking dish over medium-high heat, stir in the lemon juice and mustard, and cook until the pan juices are slightly thickened, about 3 minutes.

Arrange 3 fish slices on each plate and top with the vegetables and pan juices. Garnish with the fresh basil leaves and serve immediately.

Serves 4 as a main course.

1 cup shelled fresh fava beans
2 pounds white fish fillet, skinned
    and cut on the diagonal across
    the grain into 12 equal slices
    about 1 inch thick
Salt
Freshly ground black pepper
1 cup shelled fresh or thawed frozen
    green peas
2 tablespoons finely minced fresh basil
½ cup firm but ripe tomato, peeled
    and chopped
¼ cup fruity olive oil, preferably
    extra-virgin
3 tablespoons dry white wine
2 tablespoons freshly squeezed lemon
    juice
1 tablespoon Dijon-style mustard
Fresh basil sprigs for garnish

Baked Seared Fish
with Asparagus Salad

LEMON HERB VINAIGRETTE
About 3 tablespoons freshly squeezed
    lemon juice
2 tablespoons chopped fresh herbs
    such as chervil, chives, or
    parsley, preferably flat-leaf
    type, one kind or a combination
1 teaspoon pink pepperberries
    (optional)
About ½ teaspoon sugar (optional)
About ¼ teaspoon salt
About ¼ teaspoon freshly ground
    white pepper
½ cup fruity olive oil, preferably
    extra-virgin

1 pound very thin asparagus
2 pounds firm-fleshed or flaky-fleshed
    fish fillet, with attractive skin,
    cut into 4 equal pieces
Salt
Freshly ground white pepper
Unsalted butter for searing and
    greasing
Pink pepperberries for garnish
    (optional)
Shredded pesticide-free rose petals
    for garnish (optional)

This basic cooking method can be successfully adapted to many other serving suggestions. For example, in place of the asparagus and vinaigrette, prepare the fish as directed and serve it with a Compound Butter (page 90) or a favorite warm sauce.

To make the vinaigrette, in a bowl or a jar with a cover, combine 3 tablespoons lemon juice, herbs, pink pepperberries (if used), sugar (if used), and salt and white pepper to taste. Whisk well or cover and shake to blend well. Add the oil and whisk or shake until emulsified. Taste and add more lemon juice if needed. Set aside.

Steam the asparagus or cook them in a large pot of salted boiling water to cover until tender-crisp and bright green. Drain and plunge into cold water to halt cooking and preserve color. Divide the asparagus into 4 equal portions. On a cutting board, arrange the tops of the spears of each portion in a triangular pattern, with the tallest spear in the center. Cut the bottoms of the stalks on the diagonal to match the tops, as shown in the photograph. Set aside.

Preheat an oven to 450° F.

Quickly rinse the fish under cold running water and pat dry with paper toweling. Season to taste with salt and pepper.

In a sauté pan or skillet over medium-high heat, melt 2 tablespoons butter. Add a piece of fish, skin side down, press it down with a spatula, and sear until the skin is very crisp, about 2 minutes. Transfer the fish, skin side up, to a greased baking sheet. Wipe the pan and add additional butter as required for searing the rest of the fish. Transfer the baking sheet to the preheated oven and bake until the flesh is opaque when cut into at the thickest part with a small, sharp knife, about 4 minutes, or until done to preference.

To serve, arrange the asparagus portions on 4 individual plates and spoon the vinaigrette over the top. Place the fish, skin side up, atop the asparagus. Garnish with pink pepperberries (if used) and rose petals (if used) and serve immediately.

Serves 4 as a main course.

Zucchini-Scaled Baked Fish Fillet with Dijon Carrot Sauce

DIJON CARROT SAUCE
¼ cup (½ stick) unsalted butter, or
    3 tablespoons light olive oil
3 tablespoons all-purpose flour
2 cups freshly extracted or purchased
    carrot juice (from about
    4 carrots, if using a juice
    extractor)
¼ cup dry white wine
¼ cup (½ stick) unsalted butter
1 teaspoon Dijon-style mustard
⅛ teaspoon ground cinnamon
⅛ teaspoon freshly grated nutmeg
Salt
Ground cayenne pepper
2 tablespoons minced fresh mint

3 or 4 zucchini, very thinly sliced into
    rounds
4 whole fish fillets, about 8 ounces
    each, skinned
Salt
Freshly ground black pepper
6 tablespoons (¾ stick) unsalted
    butter, melted, or light olive oil
Dry white wine or water
Fresh mint sprigs for garnish
Thinly sliced carrot rounds, cooked
    until tender-crisp, for plate
    garnish (optional)

Although almost any fish can be used, flat fish such as flounder or sole are the perfect choices for this dish.

To make the carrot sauce, melt the butter or heat the oil in a saucepan over medium heat. Add the flour and cook, stirring, about 3 minutes; do not brown. Slowly whisk in the carrot juice until smooth. Blend in the wine, butter, mustard, cinnamon, nutmeg, and salt and cayenne pepper to taste and cook until the sauce is the consistency of heavy cream. Remove from the heat and stir in the mint. Set aside; reheat before serving.

Parboil the zucchini in salted boiling water until just beginning to soften. Drain and plunge into cold water to halt cooking. Drain well and set aside.

Preheat an oven to 450° F.

Quickly rinse the fish under cold running water and pat dry with paper toweling. Season to taste with salt and pepper. Brush the fish lightly with melted butter or oil. Lay the zucchini rounds diagonally across the fish to cover the fish entirely, overlapping the slices slightly. Brush the zucchini all over with the melted butter or oil.

In a shallow baking pan or a baking sheet with a high rim, pour in wine or water to a depth of ⅛ inch. Place the vegetable-covered fish in the liquid. Bake until the flesh is opaque when cut into at the thickest part with a small, sharp knife, about 10 minutes per inch of thickness, or until done to preference.

To serve, reheat the sauce and ladle a portion onto each plate. Top each pool of sauce with a fish fillet. Float the mint sprigs in the sauce and garnish the plate rims with carrot rounds (if used). Serve immediately.

Serves 4 as a main course.

Parchment-Wrapped Fish

Six 10- by 20-inch rectangles of
    baking parchment or heavy-
    duty butcher paper
Softened unsalted butter or high-
    quality vegetable oil
2 small carrots, peeled and cut into
    very thin julienne
2 green onions, including some of the
    green tops, cut into very thin
    julienne
1 cup fresh, thawed frozen, or drained
    canned corn kernels
½ large red sweet pepper, cut into
    very thin julienne
1 or 2 small fresh hot chiles such as
    serrano or jalapeño, cut into
    very thin julienne
½ cup coarsely chopped fresh cilantro
    (coriander)
6 firm-fleshed or flaky-fleshed fish
    steaks, about 8 ounces *each* and
    1 inch thick, or 3 pounds fish
    fillet, skinned and cut into
    6 equal pieces
6 tablespoons tequila
6 tablespoons freshly squeezed lime
    juice
3 tablespoons unsalted butter, melted
Salt
Ground dried hot chile, preferably
    ancho or pasilla
6 thin lime slices
Fresh cilantro sprigs for garnish

Diners are greeted by aromatic bursts of southwestern flavors when they cut these puffed packets open with a sharp knife. The rest of the meal should be completely ready so that the packets can go directly from the oven to the table. The only problem with this cooking method is the inability to test the fish to see if it is done; you'll have to rely on measuring the thickness of the fish beforehand and cooking it 10 minutes per inch for completely opaque fish, or a little less if you prefer moister fish. Choose firm-fleshed or flaky-fleshed fish for this method; soft-fleshed fish cooks too quickly.

Preheat an oven to 475° F.

Rub one side of each sheet of paper lightly with butter or vegetable oil and fold the paper in half to form a square with greased sides facing each other. Set aside.

In a bowl, combine the carrots, onions, corn, sweet pepper, chiles, and chopped cilantro. Open the greased paper and scatter half of the mixture evenly over one side of each piece of parchment, leaving at least a 2-inch border on all 4 sides.

Quickly rinse the fish under cold running water and pat dry with paper toweling. Place a piece of fish on top of the vegetables on each piece of paper.

In a small bowl, stir together the tequila and lime juice. Spoon 2 tablespoons of the mixture over each piece of fish. Drizzle the fish evenly with the melted butter and sprinkle with salt and ground chile to taste. Place a lime slice on each piece of fish and scatter the remaining vegetable mixture evenly over the top.

Fold the other half of the paper over the fish and seal each packet securely by making a series of tight overlapping folds along each side to form a square. Place the packets on a baking sheet and bake until the packets puff up, about 10 minutes. Immediately transfer the packets to individual plates, garnish with the cilantro sprigs, and serve.

Serves 6 as a main course.

Southeast Asian Fish Packets

In Southeast Asia fish packets like these are usually made with banana leaves. If you live near a market that specializes in Southeast Asian groceries, you may find banana leaves in the freezer section, or the local florist may get fresh banana fronds from a tropical importer. Those who live in warm environs or have a greenhouse can grow banana palms. In lieu of banana leaves, less aromatic (and certainly less glamorous) aluminum foil can be used to seal in the fish juices and the simple yet tasty ingredients.

Rich oily fish such as bonito, butterfish, large herring, mackerel, and salmon are the best choices for this preparation. Just about any fish can be used, however.

If using fresh banana leaves, place the pieces in a bowl, add boiling water to cover, and let stand until softened, about 5 minutes; drain and set aside. If using thawed leaves or aluminum foil, set aside.

In a food processor, blender, or mortar with a pestle, combine the green onion, garlic, ginger, 2 whole chiles, lime zest, and salt to taste and blend to a coarse paste. Set aside.

Preheat an oven to 450° F.

Quickly rinse the fish under cold running water and pat dry with paper toweling. Measure each fish or fish fillet at its thickest part and note the measurement. Rub the paste all over the fish. Place 1 fish in the middle of each square of banana leaf or aluminum foil. Strew the cilantro, lime slices, and slivered chiles over the fish. Wrap the leaves around the fish, then pinch each end together and fold it back over the fish. Tie the packets in several places with narrow strips of softened banana leaf or with cotton string. If using aluminum foil, wrap it around the fish, then twist each end together; do not tie.

Place the packets on a baking sheet and bake 10 minutes per inch of thickness for completely opaque flesh, or a little less for moister fish. Serve immediately. Let diners cut the packets open at the table.

Serves 4 as a main course.

4 pieces fresh or thawed frozen banana leaves, cut into 12-inch squares, or aluminum foil, cut to the same dimension
Boiling water, if using fresh leaves
½ cup coarsely chopped green onion, including some of the green tops
4 garlic cloves
4 thin slices fresh ginger root
2 small fresh green hot chiles, seeded if desired
Zest of 1 lime
About 1 teaspoon salt
Four 10- to 12-ounce whole-dressed fish, or 2 pounds fish fillet, cut into 4 equal pieces
12 fresh cilantro sprigs
8 thin lime slices, cut in half
2 small fresh red or green hot chiles, cut into julienne strips

Roasted Fish in a Lemon-Nut Crust

Here a venerable cooking method is updated with the sprightly flavors of lemon, herbs, and chopped nuts. The result is moist fish with a crunchy coating.

Serve with Old-Fashioned Tartar Sauce (page 93), a sweet-hot mustard, or fresh salsa.

Preheat an oven to 550° F.

In a shallow bowl, combine the nuts, bread crumbs, minced thyme, and lemon zest. Pour the milk into a second shallow bowl. Set the crumb mixture and milk aside.

Quickly rinse the fish under cold running water and pat dry with paper toweling. Season to taste with salt and pepper. Dip each piece of the fish into the milk and then into the crumb mixture to cover completely; with your fingertips, pat the fish all over so that the crumbs are well adhered.

Set a rack on a baking sheet and brush the rack with vegetable oil. Arrange the fish without touching on the rack and drizzle the butter or oil over the fish. Bake on an upper shelf of the oven until golden on the outside and the flesh is opaque when cut into at the thickest part with a small, sharp knife, about 10 minutes per inch of thickness, or until done to preference.

Transfer the fish pieces to individual serving plates or a platter. Garnish with the lemon zest and greens or herb sprigs. Serve hot.

Serves 4 as a main course.

½ cup finely chopped toasted pecans, hazelnuts (filberts), or other nuts
½ cup fine dry bread crumbs, preferably made from French bread
¼ cup minced fresh thyme, preferably lemon thyme, or 2 tablespoons crumbled dried thyme
1 tablespoon freshly minced or grated lemon zest
1 cup milk
2 pounds fish fillet, skinned and cut into 8 equal pieces
Salt
Freshly ground black pepper
Vegetable oil for brushing
¾ cup (1½ sticks) unsalted butter, melted, or ½ cup fruity olive oil, preferably extra-virgin
Fresh lemon zest, cut into very thin julienne, for garnish
Mizuna or other greens, or fresh thyme, preferably lemon variety, or other herb sprigs for garnish

Roasted Whole Fish

One 5- to 6-pound whole-dressed
    fish, boned
Salt
Freshly ground black pepper
About 12 fresh herb sprigs, such as
    dill, fennel, oregano, or thyme
1 or 2 lemons, thinly sliced
Vegetable oil for brushing
About ¼ pound (1 stick) unsalted
    butter, melted
6 or more cups assorted vegetables,
    cooked separately and kept
    warm (see recipe introduction)
Fresh herb sprigs (same as used to
    stuff fish) for garnish

On a large platter, surround this whole succulent fish with a variety of vegetables in various colors and shapes. Consider cherry tomatoes sautéed in garlic butter, steamed green beans or asparagus, crisply cooked peas, glazed baby carrots, tiny yellow squash, and roasted new potatoes or fried potato slices.

Choose fish with colorful skins or interesting shapes such as black sea bass, bluefish, pompano, red snapper, or striped bass.

Serve with Beurre Blanc (page 90), a fresh tomato sauce, or another favorite warm sauce.

Preheat an oven to 450° F. Lightly oil a wire rack large enough to hold the fish. Set the rack on a baking sheet.

Quickly rinse the fish under cold running water and pat dry with paper toweling. Lightly season the cavity with salt and pepper and stuff it with the herb sprigs and lemon slices. Insert small metal skewers through the edges of the cavity and lace with cotton string to secure the fish and keep the stuffing in place, or sew the cavity closed with cotton thread. If desired, score the fish in several places for more even cooking. To determine the cooking time, measure the fish at its thickest point and note the measurement.

Place the fish on the prepared rack. Brush the fish all over with the melted butter. Roast until the flesh is opaque when cut into at the thickest part with a small, sharp knife, about 10 minutes per inch of thickness, or until done to preference.

Remove the fish from the oven to a serving platter and remove the string and skewers or thread. Arrange the cooked vegetables attractively around the fish. Garnish with herb sprigs and serve immediately.

Serves 6 as a main course.

SAUCES & CONDIMENTS

Properly cooked fish often needs no more than a squeeze of fresh lemon and a drizzle of melted butter or olive oil. A delicate or robust sauce can, however, add considerable interest and create a welcome change from the ordinary.

Here are a few classic sauces for both hot and cold fish dishes. Some have been suggested in the preceding pages to accompany a particular cooking presentation. Feel free to match those that intrigue you with any of the recipes in this volume.

Beurre Blanc

An absolute classic with grilled, broiled, or roasted fish.

6 tablespoons minced shallot
6 tablespoons dry white wine
2 tablespoons freshly squeezed lemon
    juice or white wine vinegar
½ cup (1 stick) unsalted butter, cut
    into 8 equal pieces
Salt
Freshly ground black pepper

In a nonreactive saucepan over medium-high heat, combine the shallot, wine, and lemon juice or vinegar. Cook until the shallot is tender but not too dark and the liquid has reduced to about 2 tablespoons, about 6 minutes; avoid scorching the shallot.

Remove the pan from the heat and add 1 piece of the butter, stirring with a wooden spoon or wire whisk until the butter melts. Place the pan over low heat and add the remaining butter, 1 piece at a time, stirring each time until the butter melts before adding the next piece. When all the butter has been added, season to taste with salt and pepper. Serve immediately or place in a double boiler over barely simmering water for up to 30 minutes.

Makes about ½ cup, enough for about 4 servings.

VARIATION: To make *beurre rouge*, use red wine and red wine vinegar.

Compound Butter

Choose one or a pleasing combination of the suggested additions.

¼ pound (1 stick) unsalted butter,
    softened

ADDITIONS
2 tablespoons minced fresh herb,
    such as basil, chives, cilantro
    (coriander), dill, or tarragon
2 teaspoons minced fresh ginger root
    or garlic
1 teaspoon prepared mustard or
    horseradish
2 teaspoons chopped drained capers
1 teaspoon minced canned anchovy
    fillet
2 tablespoons freshly squeezed lemon
    or lime juice, or 2 teaspoons
    freshly grated lemon or lime zest,
    or to taste
Salt
Freshly ground black or white
    pepper, or ground cayenne pepper

In a bowl with a wooden spoon or in an electric mixer, food processor, or blender, beat the butter until light and fluffy. Add 1 or a combination of the suggested additions and season to taste with salt and pepper; mix well. Cover and chill for at least 1 hour before serving, or store for up to 5 days. Return almost to room temperature before serving. Serve as dollops, scrape into curls, roll into balls, or cut into pats or shapes.

To serve as a hot sauce, melt the flavored butter in a small saucepan and pour over the fish just before serving.

Makes about ½ cup, enough for about 4 servings.

Herbed Cream

Select a plentiful herb to flavor this luxurious topping for fish.

2 cups heavy (whipping) cream
1½ cups minced or shredded fresh
    herb such as basil, cilantro
    (coriander), dill, sorrel, tarragon,
    or watercress
Freshly squeezed lemon juice
Salt
Freshly ground white pepper

Combine the cream and 1 cup of the herb in a small saucepan over low heat. Simmer until the cream is reduced to half, about 20 minutes.

Pour the cream mixture through a wire sieve set over a small bowl, pressing against the herb with the back of a wooden spoon to release all liquid. Stir in the remaining ½ cup of the herb and season to taste with lemon juice, salt, and pepper. Reheat gently and serve immediately.

Makes about 1½ cups, enough for 6 servings.

Rich Wine Sauce

Either white or red wine is the base for this sumptuous sauce for a special fish dish.

3 cups dry white wine or light red
    wine
½ cup minced shallot
1½ cups Fish Stock (page 36), or
    ¾ cup canned chicken broth
    diluted with ¾ cup water
3 cups heavy (whipping) cream
6 tablespoons (¾ stick) unsalted
    butter, cut into 6 equal pieces
¼ cup chopped or shredded fresh
    basil or tarragon
Freshly squeezed lemon juice
Salt
Ground cayenne pepper

In a small saucepan over medium-high heat, combine the wine and shallot. Bring to a boil and cook until the liquid is reduced to about 3 tablespoons, about 35 minutes.

Add the stock or diluted broth and continue boiling until slightly reduced, about 5 minutes. Add the cream and continue boiling until reduced to about 1¾ cups, about 30 minutes. Reduce the heat to low and add the butter, 1 piece at a time, stirring with a wooden spoon or wire whisk until each piece melts before adding the next piece. When all the butter has been added, stir in the basil or tarragon and lemon juice, salt, and cayenne pepper to taste. Serve immediately.

Makes about 2 cups, enough for 8 servings.

Amandine Sauce

Luxurious over deep-fried or panfried fish. Chopped pecans, walnuts, or other nuts may be used in place of the almonds.

1 cup (2 sticks) unsalted butter
2 tablespoons freshly squeezed lemon
    juice
¾ cup sliced almonds or slivered
    blanched almonds
About ½ teaspoon salt
About ½ teaspoon freshly ground
    black pepper
2 tablespoons minced fresh parsley,
    preferably flat-leaf type

In a heavy saucepan over low heat, melt the butter and cook until the butter begins to brown. Stir in the lemon juice, almonds, and salt and pepper to taste. Cook until the almonds are fragrant and browned. Remove from the heat and stir in the parsley. Serve immediately.

Makes about 1½ cups, enough for 6 servings.

Herbed Mayonnaise

Use one herb or a combination. Basil, dill, and tarragon each impart a strong flavor and should be used alone or in combination with milder herbs such as chervil or parsley.

1 whole egg, at room temperature
1 egg yolk, at room temperature
1 teaspoon Dijon-style mustard
1½ tablespoons freshly squeezed
    lemon juice, or more to taste
1 cup safflower or other vegetable oil
Salt
½ to 1 cup minced fresh herbs (see
    recipe introduction)

In a blender or food processor, combine the whole egg, egg yolk, mustard, and lemon juice. Blend for about 30 seconds. With the motor running at high speed, pour in the oil in a slow, steady stream. When the mayonnaise thickens to a creamy consistency, turn off the motor. With a rubber or plastic spatula, scrape down any oil from the sides of the container and blend it into the mayonnaise. Taste and add salt and more lemon juice, if desired.

Transfer the mayonnaise to a bowl. Add the herbs and mix well with a wooden spoon or wire whisk. Transfer to a covered container and refrigerate for at least 2 hours before serving, or store for up to 2 days. Return almost to room temperature before serving; whisk to blend if it separates.

Makes about 1½ cups, enough for 6 servings.

Garlic Mayonnaise

Based on classic Mediterranean *aioli,* this creamy sauce is excellent with cold or hot fish.

4 garlic cloves, or to taste
2 egg yolks, at room temperature
¼ teaspoon Dijon-style mustard
1½ tablespoons freshly squeezed
    lemon juice
1 cup plus 3 tablespoons olive oil
Salt
Freshly ground white pepper

In a blender or food processor, mince the garlic. Add the egg yolks, mustard, and lemon juice and blend for about 30 seconds. With the motor running at high speed, add the oil in a slow, steady steam. When the sauce thickens to a creamy consistency, turn off the motor. With a rubber or plastic spatula, scrape down any oil from the sides of the container and blend it into the sauce. Season to taste with salt and pepper.

Use the sauce immediately or transfer it to a covered container and refrigerate for up to 2 days. Return the sauce almost to room temperature before serving; whisk to blend if it separates.

Makes about 1½ cups, enough for 6 servings.

Red Pepper Sauce (*Rouille*)

Stir into a fish soup or use as a condiment for grilled or baked fish.

2 red sweet peppers
¾ cup fine fresh bread crumbs, made
    from French bread with crust
    removed
About ¼ cup Fish Stock (page 36) or
    2 tablespoons canned chicken
    broth diluted with 2 tablespoons
    water
4 garlic cloves
2 tablespoons fruity olive oil,
    preferably extra-virgin
Salt
Freshly ground black pepper

Roast the peppers over a charcoal fire or an open gas flame or place under a preheated broiler. Turn the peppers several times until their skin is charred on all sides. Place the peppers in a loosely closed paper bag to cool for about 10 minutes. With your fingertips, rub away the charred skin. Cut each pepper in half, seed, devein, and coarsely chop.

Place the chopped peppers in a food processor, blender, or mortar. Add all of the remaining ingredients, except the salt and pepper, and blend or grind to a thick paste. If the sauce is too thick, add a little more stock or broth. Season to taste with salt and pepper.

Makes about 2 cups, enough for 8 servings.

Remoulade

A French tradition with cold fish.

⅓ cup homemade mayonnaise or
    high-quality commercial
    mayonnaise
¼ cup Creole or Dijon-style mustard
¼ cup high-quality vegetable oil
1 tablespoon freshly squeezed lemon
    juice or cider vinegar
1 tablespoon prepared white
    horseradish
2 tablespoons minced fresh parsley
1½ teaspoons minced fresh tarragon
1½ teaspoons minced gherkins
1½ teaspoons drained capers,
    chopped
½ teaspoon minced or pressed garlic
2 flat canned anchovy fillets, minced,
    or ½ teaspoon anchovy paste
1 tablespoon sweet paprika
Salt
Freshly ground black pepper
Liquid hot-pepper sauce

In a small bowl, combine the
mayonnaise, mustard, oil, lemon juice
or vinegar, and horseradish. Blend well.
Stir in the parsley, tarragon, gherkins,
capers, garlic, anchovy, and paprika.
Season to taste with salt, pepper, and
pepper sauce. Transfer to a covered
container and refrigerate for at least 2
hours before serving, or store for up to
4 days.

**Makes about 1¼ cups, enough for 4
servings.**

Old-Fashioned Tartar Sauce

Some people rate this standby as
indispensible with fried fish. Freshly
made it beats any bottled version that
I've tried.

1 cup homemade mayonnaise or
    high-quality commercial
    mayonnaise
½ cup minced dill pickle
2 tablespoons minced green onion,
    including some of the green tops
2 tablespoons minced fresh parsley
2 teaspoons minced capers
1 tablespoon freshly squeezed lemon
    juice
1 teaspoon Worcestershire sauce
About ¼ teaspoon salt
About ¼ teaspoon freshly ground
    black pepper
About ⅛ teaspoon ground cayenne
    pepper

In a small bowl, combine all of the
ingredients and mix well. Cover and
refrigerate for at least 1 hour or for up
to 2 days. Return almost to room
temperature before serving; whisk to
blend if the sauce separates.

**Makes about 1½ cups, enough for 6
servings.**

Citrus Salsa

This tangy, sweet condiment goes great
with spicy grilled, broiled, or baked
fish.

1 large grapefruit, preferably pink
2 large oranges or tangerines
½ cup minced fresh mint
3 tablespoons minced fresh chives
2 tablespoons freshly squeezed lemon
    or lime juice
1 teaspoon granulated sugar
¼ teaspoon Tabasco sauce or other
    liquid hot-pepper sauce, or to
    taste
Salt

Peel the grapefruit and oranges or
tangerines. Section the fruits and
remove all of the white pith and
membrane. Coarsely chop the fruits and
place them in a colander set over a
bowl. Let drain for about 5 minutes.

Transfer the drained fruits to a bowl.
Add all of the remaining ingredients,
including the salt to taste. Stir to
combine well, cover, and chill for about
1 hour or for up to several hours.

**Makes about 3 cups, enough for 6 to
8 servings.**

INDEX

RECIPE INDEX

INDEX TO FISH RECIPES IN OTHER JAMES McNAIR COOKBOOKS

ACKNOWLEDGMENTS

The fish chair used in my portrait and the dishes on pages 1, 37, 68, 89, and 96 were made and provided by MacKenzie-Childs, available at Neiman-Marcus and other fine stores.

Plates on pages 25, 46, 62, and 83 were made and provided by Cyclamen Studios, available at fine stores everywhere.

Plates on pages 4, 50, 52, 66, and 71 were provided by Fillamento, San Francisco.

Plates on pages 30, 79, and 81 are from the collection of Dishes Delmar, San Francisco.

Vintage tuna bakers on page 74 are from the collection of Tom Worthington.

Recipes were tested by Janice Blake, Ruth Dosher, Gail and Tad High, Jim Hildreth, Dorothy Knecht, Connie Landry, Debbie Matsumoto, Marian May, Scottie McKinney, J. O. and Lucille McNair, Martha McNair, Tom and Nancy Riess, Babs Retzer, John Richardson, Alice and Billy Russell-Shapiro, Bob and Kristi Spence, Bert Tessler, Sabrina Vasquez, Kathryn Wittenmeyer, and Sharon Woo.

To Chronicle Books for their continued good work with my series.

To copyeditor Sharon Silva for once again smoothing out all the rough places.

To my assistant Ellen Berger-Quan for painting the backgrounds in addition to her usual countless duties.

To Jim Hildreth for answering all my questions as I photographed my first solo book.

To Russ Fischella for the creative portrait session.

To Tom Worthington of the Monterey Fish Market for his expert advice and for securing the fish for testing and photography.

To John Carr for the generous loan of his house as a photo studio.

To Scottie McKinney for cutting so many of her edible flowers.

To Larry Heller for all of his help in setting up my new computer system.

To Cleve Gallat and Samantha Schwemler of CTA Graphics for their terrific typesetting and mechanicals.

To my family and friends for their constant encouragement, especially to Martha and Devereux McNair, Mark Leno, and John Richardson for providing nonfish culinary experiences during production of this book, and to my parents, James and Lucille McNair, for introducing me to fish and providing Louisiana catfish whenever they arrive for a visit.

To my loyal companions Addie Prey, Buster Booroo, Joshua J. Chew, Michael T. Wigglebutt, and Dweasel Pickle. And a special welcome to our gang for Beauregard Ezekiel "Zeke" Valentine!

To my partner Lin Cotton for pushing and pulling me along through it all, and especially for his refusal to accept no as an answer to the idea of adding photography to my other duties on these books.